# THE BUSINESS
# OF
# GIFT BASKETS

## How To Make A Profit Working From Home

Camille Anderson & Don L. Price

**Those Bloomin' Baskets, etc.**
*by Camille Anderson*

**P.O. Box 7000-B&B**
**Redondo Beach, CA 90277**
**310•316•0611**

# THE BUSINESS OF GIFT BASKETS
*How To Make A Profit Working From Home*

Published by
**Price/Anderson**

Copyright © 1991 by Camille Anderson and Don L. Price
First printing 1991
Printed in the United States of America

**Library of Congress Card Catalog Data:**

The Business of Gift Baskets, How to make a profit working from home
Library of Congress Card Catalog Number: 91-091375
ISBN Number: 0-9630396-2-8

Book design and layout by ONE-ON ONE BOOK DESIGN

Cover design by ONE-ON-ONE BOOK DESIGN and FIZZ GRAPHICS

*This book is dedicated to Camille's daughter Shannon
and Don's daughters Keri and Kristy.
We love and support your dreams of happiness, health and prosperity.*

# ACKNOWLEDGMENT

We wish to express our sincere thanks and appreciation to our beloved family and friends who shared so much of their precious time in reading our manuscript. Their comments and suggestions were invaluable to the success of this book. Vi Anderson, George Trippon, Connie Ingersoll, Mike McCarty, Meme Amaral, Lee Gardner, Janelle Burrill, John M. O'Donnell, Philip Simenton and Barbara Wold — thank you all dearly for your words of wisdom and generous support.

We thank Carolyn Porter, ONE-ON-ONE BOOK DESIGN, for her patience in editing and helping us through the editing/production process. Her creative talent for design and layout gives this book the added dimension that makes it come alive.

We are especially grateful to Ruth Planey for her talented writing skills in helping us add levity and for her many brilliant ideas she contributed to help make this a better book for all to read.

# ABOUT THE AUTHORS

**C**amille Anderson is founder and owner of *Those Bloomin' Baskets, etc.*; a unique service providing custom designed and personalized gift baskets. She opened her business in 1981 and has been featured at some of California's finest wineries including a special invitation to display her designer baskets at the famous Domaine Chandon. Her client list reads like a who's who from politicians and athletes to presidents of corporations. Her ten years in business along with her love of creating gift baskets has been the inspiration for writing this book.

**D**on L. Price is a dynamic and inspiring professional speaker, business consultant and seminar leader. He has extensive experience and expertise in sales training, marketing, and corporate management in the financial, retail and service industries. He conducts various training programs covering how to set up a successful home-based business, how to sell products through seminars, and the art of customer service through effective communications.

# Table of Contents

# INTRODUCTION

This book was written for the all of you who would like to start your own business and for those of you who would like to know more about creating baskets for gift-giving. Many people try to start their own business with little knowledge or skills in sales and marketing. Without these skills the business may never get off the ground. Through our experience in the gift basket business, we know the rewards as well as the pitfalls — and that is what this book is all about.

*Those Bloomin' Baskets, etc.*, has been in operation since 1981. It started with a single concept of providing picnic baskets that were both functional and decorative — and, successfully expanded into a line of gift baskets offering a diversity of themes along with custom design.

The '90s is an opportune time to earn more money by becoming an independent specialty business owner — and gift baskets will always be "in." Now is the time to become a part of a growing number of men and women across America who have chosen to work out of the home, making entrepreneurship a major career option. This book can be your guide to a full-time or part-time business based on the success of *Those Bloomin' Baskets, etc.*

We would like to mention here some of the character traits and skills that help a small business owner become a successful entrepreneur.

* An adventuresome spirit and willingness to take risks

* An optimistic attitude, energy and enthusiasm

* Resourcefulness

* Honesty and integrity

* Good people skills and communication skills

* Creativity, whether natural or learned.

* Good managerial planning and organizational skills

* Any business experience is an asset, however it is not a prerequisite. The knowledge of finance, keeping records and books can be acquired.

* Self-discipline — the ability to separate business hours from domestic responsibilities and personal pleasures

* Perseverance — the ability to stick to a project and see it through to the end

* Motivation

* Flexibility, willingness to change your schedule to meet needs as they arise.

* Self-confidence and high self-esteem

## How to Use the Book

We have endeavored to present the information in a logical manner and realize that some information already may be a part of your expertise. Therefore, you may want to skip over a chapter and head for the information that will be most helpful to you. Rather than list resources in the appropriate chapters, we felt it would be more convenient for you to access the list from Appendix B. You will note, as you read through the book, that there is sub-text (indicated by an indent and different typestyle) to share our personal experiences and give extra tips.

**"THE BUSINESS OF GIFT BASKETS"** is full of good ideas and information and it is our sincere hope that it will help and inspire you to get into the gift basket business.

**Chapter 1**

# $A$BOUT THE GIFT BASKET BUSINESS

$S$ hopping convenience is a priority because most people work and working people lack the time to browse for that *special gift* for that *special person*, client, etc. Now you, as a gift basket designer and business owner, can watch your profits grow as you fulfill the need for just the right gifts for your clientele.

The decade of the '90s represents a popular career option of owning your own business and working from your home. This book will introduce and thoroughly explain everything you need to know to become an entrepreneur in a unique business that meets the needs of the customer and where the number one goals are quality and service — *The Specialty Gift Basket Business*.

Gift baskets are popular and they are here to stay! It has been proven over and over again that people will pay to have someone do tasks they either dislike or for which they need help. And when it comes to shopping, many busy people just simply do not have the time and energy. That is why the potential in this specialty gift basket business is unlimited.

*"Entrepreneurs are filling baskets not only with food, but with everything from antique picture frames to baby clothes. ...and with the average gift basket selling for $40 and prices escalating as high as $500, profits are not just a drop in the basket."*
　　　　　　—Lisa Hughes Anderson, New Business Opportunities, January 1991.

# Benefits of a Home-based Gift Basket Business

The benefits of becoming a gift basket entrepreneur are varied and far-reaching. Once you see the positive way it can enhance your personal life and economic future, you will be anxious to create your first custom basket.

**Economic Savings**. Low start-up costs and a minimal amount of equipment keep the initial costs down so you can get established more easily, turn a profit sooner, and increase your chances of success. Overhead is kept down because there is no monthly rent for an office or retail store to pay. Just use the extra space in your own home — a garage or extra closet space — to save money on storage. The money that you save on rent and storage can be used to build your inventory.

Can you imagine all of the other expenses that you would incur if your business was located off the premises? The amount of money you will save in transportation alone is incredible (not to mention the numerous headaches you no longer have to endure stuck in commuter traffic if you decide to operate this business full time). You will not need to spend major amounts of money on appropriate office clothing anymore. Wear anything you want except when you call on corporate accounts — then, of course, dressing for success is important. For those of you who have children, you will be amazed at what you no longer have to spend on child care.

**Be Your Own Boss**. Working from home means more control over your schedule and your environment. *You are in charge*. There is no boss standing over your shoulder. There is no time clock to punch. Leave the corporate structure and demands behind you. Take a vacation when it appeals to you. Make your own decisions about purchasing inventory, pricing your baskets, and conducting operations. The success of this business is 100% what you, the person in charge, make of it.

**Set Your Own Hours.** It is certainly a viable option to run a part-time gift basket business and hold down a regular job at the same time if you so desire. This flexibility can suit your priorities. For example, by controlling the amount of baskets you complete each day, you can set aside anywhere from ten to fifty hours of work per week for yourself. You no longer have to arrange your life to fit the business world's nine to five routine — you arrange your business to fit your life style. Work during the hours when you feel the most productive, energetic and creative and you will accomplish a great deal more.

**Financial Independence**. When you are your own boss, the sky is the limit on your potential income. You can run a gift basket business as a part-time sideline effort that brings extra income annually, or build it into a very profitable enterprise by working at it full time. It can be a dream come true if you apply yourself and follow the simple procedures and suggestions set forth in this book.

*"…Since she began catering to corporate clients in 1987, her profits have doubled each year; she expects 1991 profits to be more than $100,000."*
— New Business Opportunities, January 1991

**Achieve Pride and Prestige.** There is nothing like feeling the pride and prestige that one achieves in becoming an independent business owner.

*"…Launching your own business is like writing your own personal declaration of independence from the corporate beehive… Becoming an entrepreneur is the modern-day equivalent of pioneering on the old frontier."*
— Paula Nelson

**Creative Freedom**. You can now fully utilize your skills and knowledge to work and be paid. Gift basket designing is creative and you can learn this skill.

**Tax advantages**. If you meet IRS requirements, you can turn personal expenses such as rent, furniture and telephone costs into tax-deductible items. At this time, the Internal Revenue Service lets you deduct part of the costs of operating your home-based business provided the space used is solely for your business. Other deductions are discussed in detail in Appendix A.

Most entrepreneurs are not adequately prepared to go into business on their own. Although they have the motivation, desire and talent, many do not take the enormous amount of time involved to properly investigate and research the business they are interested in starting. That is why so many small business owners fail in their efforts to achieve financial independence. But now, you can acquire the knowledge and skills to run a profitable gift basket business just by reading this book. We have done all the time-consuming research for you.

By being in the home-based, Specialty Gift Basket Business, you will reap the rewards of proprietorship in an industry that is growing at a rapid pace and showing strong profit potential. This innovative and unique approach to gift giving is a definite upward trend in the retail industry. Not only will you have the independence of running your own business but you will also benefit from the proven sales techniques, and the creative and technical know-how that author Camille Anderson has accrued since 1981 with her own gift basket business. The aim of this book is to share this valuable information and impart the knowledge that is essential to getting you off to a fast start into your own home-based business.

## The Business of Gift Baskets — A Good Choice

The retail environment is changing drastically. Autonomy and individuality are strengths that will serve you well as an independent business owner. You do not have to start out worrying about overhead costs that department and upscale stores are confronted with from day one of opening their doors. Some department stores do not have the time to concentrate on unique specialty items, unless they have a specialty department. The department stores that no longer promote special categories can only help the proprietor of the specialized gift basket business. Many retailers and florists are very interested in gift baskets as a real money-maker. It all boils down to one thing — gift baskets are bringing in profits.

*"One of the three fastest growing small businesses of the '90s that got its start in the '80s will continue to boom — gift baskets."*
— Steve Crowley, Money Editor

The optimistic outlook for you is geared toward meeting the demand of the consumers' buying habits. Consumers are having a long-term love affair with baskets because of the aura of romance, intrigue and old world charm. Faraway places where the bamboo, willow, rattan, and reeds come from, or thinking about the original purpose that the basket was used for years ago can become an integral part of your finished product. Consumers enjoy the naturalness of the weave, the variety of shapes and sizes and the excitement of knowing that baskets make a wonderful decorative piece in the home.

Also, another important appeal of baskets is their utility. Consumers seek new ways of using baskets, and it is our job as the seller to inform them as to the many uses of the baskets we create. This alone will definitely increase profits in your Specialty Gift Basket Business.

Above all, we have learned by listening to our customers' needs. Camille found her success in evaluating her customers' wants and then creating a quality product that fulfilled their needs. You too will learn the successful formula for creating and personalizing baskets that SELL. Just turn the pages and follow one step at a time — this comprehensive guide to learning the gift basket business from "A to Z." You are definitely in step with success as you enter into a business that has phenomenal potential for growth dictated by the mood of the '90s

*"To be successful in the business, you need to have a creative flair, a good sense of business, be people-oriented and be able to sell yourself."*
— Lisa Hughes Anderson, Gift Basket Headquarters

**Chapter 2**

# SETTING UP A GIFT BASKET BUSINESS

## Finding the Best Location for Your Office

There are many procedures for setting boundaries between your home and your work. Walls, furniture, doors, windows, lighting, and curtains are all ways you can use to delineate boundaries you want to establish. How you manage your time and space — your office location, work schedules and household rules are an individual choice and it can definitely be a balancing act at times!

First — define the following areas:

- Space that will be allocated for your office work

- Storage of inventory

- Work place — where you assemble the baskets

A good idea, if you can manage it, is to set up your office as separately as possible from the rest of your house. It may be possible for you to utilize a separate structure or a separate entrance for business guests, or you might consider soundproofing your office. If you are *not* easily distracted by noise and family activity, setting up your office in the dining room is fine.

Ask yourself these questions:

☐ How much privacy do I need to work productively? Does the sound of music, T.V. or people talking in the background distract me from my work?

☐ Do I prefer to work by myself?

☐ When concentrating on a particular task, do I ask people not to disturb me?

By answering these questions, you will be able to determine what environmental setting is best for you.

Most people need the following to work effectively at home:

- An area where you can have a desk and chair to do your paper work and make phone calls

- A place where you can set up a computer, typewriter, calculator, or other equipment

- A conversation area with chairs or a couch, where you can receive customers, hold business meetings, and "close the sale"

- Space for filing cabinets, books, and reference materials such as your catalogs from suppliers, etc.

- Storage space for inventory and working materials

- Designated working area for the actual assembling of baskets, shrink wrapping, and preparation for shipping

*"Where there is clutter, there is confusion. I need to have a slot for each item, and space to work in order to be totally organized and efficient."*
— Camille J. Anderson, Strategic Space Planning

Any part of your home can be used for work space and office. You can redesign any room or part of one to make a practical work area. Here are some suggestions for utilizing the space you have:

**Spare bedroom** – This is a good choice for a home/office. If you have ample bookshelves, they can be used to display the baskets and for storage.

**Family room** – If you also have a living room, use the family room. A desk and display items for the baskets can be set up without much inconvenience.

**Living room** – Using this as an office can be an excellent choice if you are short on extra rooms. It is usually the most spacious area of the home, easily divided into a separate office space with bookcases, partitions, screens, or furniture. It is often the most formal part of the home and therefore more appropriate for creating a business image. It is very avant-garde for the busy executive to have his/her corporate office patterned after a well-designed living room with fireplace, couch and the works!

**Kitchen** – A good possibility for an office if you have a breakfast nook to use for a desk and work area. A professional image in the kitchen is possible, but often difficult because it usually is the *stomach* of household activities. However, it can be done.

**Dining room** – Another excellent choice for an office is the infrequently used dining room. An appealing aspect to meeting clients in this room is the aroma of flavored coffee brewing. Being able to sample the goodies and taste the coffee that goes along with your gift baskets is bound to whet their appetites and make a sale.

**Bedroom** – If you don't have an extra bedroom, sometimes the master bedroom is often large enough to be divided or partitioned and screened off to use as office space.

**Closets, Dressing Rooms and Storage Spaces** – These areas can be transformed to give you enough room to work or at least to store your baskets and other inventory. You can rearrange your walk-in closets, extra large closets, storage rooms, dressing rooms, or use the space beneath and along stairways. These small areas create a compact, self-contained spot, and are well out of the way when not in use.

> *We use our large walk-in closet for the storage of our inventory. It works great!*

Also, keep in mind, that you can convert a garage or an attic, basement, patio or porch with a little imagination. Use various decorating tips such as modular panel systems, wall units, screens, bookshelf dividers, accordion doors, room dividers, and such items as a *Home/Office in a Box* which is available in different wood grains and not too expensive. You most likely have a builder's outlet near you. Here in California — we have Lumberjack, Builder's Emporium, or Home Club — they carry supplies to set up an office/work space, and showroom.

Take a look at your office, work space and showroom from the viewpoint of the people who will be coming there as customers. What kind of image does it present? Consider their expectations and the statement that your showroom/office makes about you and the basket business.

*We were fortunate that shelves were already built in the homes where we lived and ran our business. The shelves were actually in the den/study room so we converted it into the "basket-room." It is amazing how you can decorate a room or entire home with baskets to present a very "warm" and welcoming environment. We created several "standard-type" baskets and "special occasion" baskets so our customers could see the wide range of choices, flexibility and quality of our work.*

## Creating Aesthetic Value

In creating the aesthetic value in your office and display room, there are many possibilities to make a small room look larger or smaller.

**To help a small room appear larger,** use wall-to-wall carpeting that is light in color, and keep your furniture and accessories simple and organized.

Off-white or pastel-colored walls will give it a more open and clean effect, especially when using simple curtains, drapes or blinds. This helps give the appearance of a larger room. Mirrors also give an illusion of making a small room appear more spacious.

**Make a large room appear smaller** by using contrasting floor and wall coverings and prominent colors. Area rugs and heavier furniture also will create this effect.

### Use Your Business to Decorate

Your "designer baskets" can be a beautiful embellishment to your home decor. Decorate your baskets with magazines, silk flowers, stuffed animals, whatever your imagination dictates.

Colors have a definite impact on the overall effect of your office and showroom. Colors actually effect anyone entering your home in a physiological and psychological way. Use warm colors (reds, oranges, yellows, browns) to arouse, awaken, and stimulate. Use cool colors (blues, greens, grays) to calm, quiet and evoke a more serene environment.

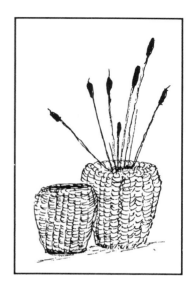

# Displaying Your Baskets

The manner you display your baskets depends on the amount of space you have. Utilize shelves in your basket room, leaving more room for furniture. Shelves are easy and fairly inexpensive to install.

Other suggestions for your display room are:

Antique furniture lends itself well to basket decor. China cabinets, armoires, chest of drawers, coat racks, hat racks, benches, desks, washbowl and stands, stoves — again, let your imagination roam and use what you already have.

Find interesting pieces for displaying baskets such as chairs, stools, ladders, wicker stands, pedestals, hatch covers (from a ship), wine or olive barrels (cut glass to fit top or drape with fabric that will enhance basket design); crates, cubes, table stacks, etageres, garden or picnic benches, even boards and bricks. Go to your local flea markets, swap meets and store closeouts to find display pieces and interesting props. The way you display the baskets definitely makes a visual statement.

*In our guest bathroom, I created a bath basket with washcloths in fancy folds, potpourri sachets, decorative soaps and baby's breath that added just the right touch and emitted a lovely peach fragrance. Each basket was also for sale and easily duplicated. A great number of our guests would want a similar basket to use in their homes.*

Aside from enjoying your own handiwork in your home, it will work to convince your customers how decorative baskets can be.

### Lighting

Lighting plays an important role in how you function in your office or work area. Lighting is critical to productivity. Natural daylight is the optimum choice for doing paperwork and creating baskets. You get your true colors in this light and that is important when designing and coordinating colors. Lighting sets the stage and focuses attention on your baskets and decor.

If natural light is not available, fluorescent or track lighting works well by evenly illuminating an area. Incandescent lighting usually comes from a single "point" source and is best used for accent lighting. Use spotlights or low voltage fixtures strategically placed to dramatically display your baskets.

String miniature white Christmas lights outlining basket shelves and other areas to create a festive, welcoming effect, especially in the evening. Use lighting to create just the right ambience to display your baskets and make your sales area unique.

## Your Business Phone

In the initial stages of setting up your business, it is acceptable to use your own home phone number. Once you get established, we recommend you set up a separate telephone line for business calls. Reasons a separate telephone line are important:

( You can make outgoing calls on one line, leaving the other free for incoming business calls.

( You can leave your personal line free for other family members to use without interfering with your business.

© Most importantly, it is much easier to claim business phone costs for tax purposes if you have two lines. (See deductions re: business phone under IRS Rules in Appendix A.)

If you add a separate line, it does not have to be a "business number" unless you want a Yellow Pages listing (see Chapter 12 under Advertising), or you need to be on file as a business with Directory Assistance. You can install a second residential line to use as your business phone.

Set up your *business* phone away from noise that might be picked up by a customer. Remember, you are a full-fledged business and want to be as professional as possible. Be formal when answering your business phone by using your company name. The way you answer the phone determines if the caller perceives you as a professional he or she can trust.

To create a positive, professional image, it is a good idea to greet callers with "Good morning" or "Good afternoon," followed by the name of your business. Your voice should radiate warmth and enthusiasm.

If other members of the family answer your business phone, instruct them to use the same professional procedure as you do.

An answering machine or an answering service is a must. You do not want to miss a client if you are out of the office, and there will be times when you need to be free from answering the phone because you are creating or concentrating on business. Choosing the machine over an answering service is more cost effective. Answering machines offer a variety of special features and differ in their capabilities. Consult a Consumer Reports Buying Guide to purchase one that suits your needs. The following features are recommended when purchasing an answering machine:

**Message review**, lets you listen to one caller without repeating the entire set of messages.

**Message counter**, lets you keep track of calls received and prevents the likelihood of lost messages.

**Remote control**, lets you check messages when you are away from home.

Here is a suggestion for a recorded message:

> "Good Morning. This is Camille and you have just reached *Those Bloomin' Baskets, etc.*, We're sorry that no one is here to answer your call personally. However, if you could please leave your name, number, time of call, and brief message, we will return your call just as soon as possible. Thank you for calling and have a nice day."

You can vary the message depending upon the time of day, season or holiday. For example, around the holidays, I like to start the message with "Happy holidays," and then continue with the rest of the message. This enhances your warmth and sincerity as a business person and, of course, your business. You want to record a professional-sounding message.

## Optional Telephone Services

&#9426; **Call forwarding** automatically transfers calls to a designated number when you are away from home so you can be reached at all times without missing that important order!

&#9426; **Call waiting** signals you if another party is trying to get through while you are talking. This lets you take the incoming call while holding the original call. This is an important feature so a customer, or potential customer, will not get frustrated with a busy signal and possibly move on to your competition. Remember, we all value our time, so if another busy person needs to order a basket, it is to your benefit to try to respond on the second or third ring. This can mean another sale.

&#9426; **Three-way calling** allows you to talk with two other people at the same time without operator assistance. This can be very advantageous when you, your partner, and a customer need to make some important decisions collectively on a large order.

## *Money and Time-Saving Ideas for Using Your Phone*

Always check your telephone bills for errors. If you find an error, the telephone company will give you credit when you draw it to its attention.

- ☎ **Touch-tone** — These phones save you time in dialing compared to rotary phones.

- ☎ **Dial direct** — This can save considerable costs not having to use operator-assisted calls.

- ☎ **Off hours** — Whenever possible, place your long-distance calls during off-hours. The rates are lower when you call before 8 am or after 5 pm on weekdays. Take advantage of time differences in placing calls to people in other areas.

- ☎ **800 numbers** are a great money saver so use them whenever that is a choice. When you are calling an out-of-town business, it is a good idea to check an 800 directory or call information: 1(800) 555-1212. Contact AT&T about ordering a business 800 directory.

- ☎ **Alternative long-distant phone companies** — Investigate all of the long-distance phone companies such as MCI or U.S. Sprint. These companies are competing for your business and might offer lower rates than AT&T. Make comparisons in their reputation for accurate billing, convenience of completing calls, broken connections and quality of sound. A number of organizations, including Consumer Reports, evaluate these services.

- ☎ **Cellular and car phones** — though expensive, they offer many advantages, especially when you are making deliveries.

- ☎ **Portable phones** — offer the convenience of being mobile and not having to run for the phone when you are out of the office and in another room.

Always have a note pad and pencil right by the phone, keep your work area organized, and try to return all calls immediately. This could mean a good order, and also a repeat customer.

# Ordering Business Cards, Letterhead, etc.

Y ou should have a unique and professional logo designed before you order your business cards, letterhead, and other business stationery needs, such as invoices. If your budget is not enough at this time to hire a graphic artist, contact a local college or training school for students in the field.

*"I found a college student who was delighted to use her talents and also get paid. I told her basically what I wanted and she took it from there. Together, we designed a fantastic logo for Those Bloomin' Baskets, etc. It depicts the nature of the business (gift baskets), and I incorporated the logo on my business cards, stationery, envelopes, invoices, gift enclosure cards, brochures, fliers, mailers, thank you notes and reminders. My clientele now associate the logo with my business. It is my "Hallmark" in the gift basket industry and it has served me well."*

— Camille J. Anderson

Your local stationery store and printer usually have a book with different graphic designs (clip art) that might work well for you and your business. Also, you can purchase software programs with graphic capabilities (some word processing programs have graphics capabilities). With this software feature, you can find the right logo or even design it yourself on your computer.

Consider the following points when designing and ordering your business cards:

- Keep the color of your business cards, stationery, envelopes, enclosure cards, reminders, and thank you notes consistent. They should all match.

- Use a quality grade of paper.

- Remember, "Simplicity is Elegance." On your business card, be sure your business name and logo stand out. Your address and phone number (with area code) need to be in a legible print style. Your business cards should depict exactly what your business is and what service it sells. Do not be vague in this area.

- Highlight customer service such as "personalized gift baskets tailored to the individual and/or occasion." You can mention theme baskets geared to all special holidays.

- You can add that you do "corporate" and employee gifts.

- Stress the fact that you work in all price ranges.

- Emphasize that "we deliver."

- Indicate that you have a professional portfolio.

A suggestion for an impressive business card is to have a good quality photo of one of your best gift baskets printed in business card size. Affix the photo to the inside of a folded business card.

*"For our business cards, we photographed a real live kitty peaking out of one of our baskets. The picture really caught attention and dramatically displayed the quality of the baskets. The saying is true, "A picture is worth a thousand words."*

— Camille J. Anderson

Adding color to your business card is also impressive but is more expensive.

# Opening Your Business Account

It is imperative that you keep your business finances separate from your personal finances. Therefore, before making any purchases for your business (supplies as well as inventory), open a business account with the name of your business. Your checks can be printed with your business name and address (usually takes two to three weeks). In the meantime, your account is open and you can keep your records straight from the start as you purchase your inventory and supplies.

Many states require you to file your fictitious business name before you open your account and you will have to take proof of filing with you. Also, some cities require a business license.

It is a good idea to look into the various types of checking accounts your bank offers. If you keep a minimum balance (this varies from bank to bank), there is usually no monthly service charge. Make sure that you can have unlimited check-writing privileges (without charge) as you will need to write many checks to purchase office supplies and inventory.

A suggested amount to start out with is $1,000. However, if you are on a very tight budget, you can do it for $500. Shop wisely for the necessary supplies to keep the cost at a minimum (see suggested Start-Up Costs at the end of this chapter).

When opening your account, make sure you have your business cards printed as the bank personnel could be one of your best customers. Be sure to inform them that you personalize and deliver the gift baskets. Take a sample basket with you and leave it in the bank as decor (attach a gift tag with your business name and extra cards inside for those people who are interested).

It is important that you write checks for all of your business purchases. This not only makes it easier for you to do the monthly bookkeeping, but also provides instant records for assembling information for tax purposes. Remember, the IRS requires records, records, and more records if you are ever audited; so you might as well start out on the right foot.

*"Losing potential profits hurts the ego; losing money really hurts."*
— Gerald Appel

# Purchasing Office Supplies

Here's a list of the basics — minimum equipment and supplies you will need:

## Supplies

| | |
|---|---|
| Accordion files for separating expenses | Paper |
| Business envelopes (same color as letterhead and business cards) | Pens, pencils, erasers, markers |
| Business cards (samples included) | Postage stamps |
| Calendar | Ring Binders |
| Computer Supplies (if you own a computer) | Rubber bands |

| | |
|---|---|
| Correction fluid (if you are going to use a typewriter) | Rubber stamps |
| File folders | Stapler and staples |
| File labels, tabs | Stationery/letterhead (samples attached) |
| Glue, rubber cement | Typewriter ribbons |
| Index cards | Paper clips |

## Small Equipment

| | |
|---|---|
| Calculator | Pencil holder |
| In and out boxes or file | Pencil sharpener |
| Letter opener | Scissors |
| Letter tray | Ruler |
| Paper cutter | Staple Remover |
| Postage scale (saves money and time) | |
| Typewriter or computer (can lease or buy a used one that has been refurbished and deduct as a business expense on your tax records) | |

If you have a good discount store such as Price Club, Costco, Office Club, or a wholesaler in your area, get your items there or at a large volume discount stationery or drug store. They all carry a wide variety of items and have reasonable return policies.

If you are thinking of purchasing a typewriter for typing invoices and correspondence, you could go one step further and invest in a personal computer and printer. In addition to carrying out highly sophisticated typing and editing functions, you can do financial computations, organize and keep records, do your inventory and keep a customer file (with dates they order, what they order, etc.). You can also draw charts, graphs, and use unique printing styles so that you can produce quality brochures, letters and forms, and even set up a spreadsheet for your budget. By doing this yourself, you can save a considerable amount of money in advertising costs.

# Start-Up Costs

**G**etting into your own business can mean a large cash investment. But starting out in the gift basket business puts very little
strain on your budget.

The following prices are based on average cost comparisons and
what we feel, through our experience in the gift basket business, is
sufficient to get you started. It is entirely possible to begin with less
initial investment if you already own some office supplies and other
equipment such as an answering machine, files, shelving, typewriter
or computer. Start-up costs will vary according to each individual.

### Start-Up Costs
### (Approximate)

* Home Office Supplies:
  - a. Postage — $ 29
  - b. Pendex Files/Manila Folders — $ 8
  - c. Staplers, Pens, Pencils, Paperclips, etc. — $ 10
  - e. Misc. i.e., Sales Receipt Book, Bookkeeping Record Book, Photo Portfolio — $ 30

  Total $ 77

* Office Equipment:
  - a. Typewriter — $ 150
  - b. Answering Machine — $ 60
  - c. Desk, File Cabinet — $ 180
  - d. Work Table (Folding or Plywood Table) — $ 40
  - e. Fax and Computer Optional (not included in start up cost) — $
  - f. Storage Bins — $ 100

  Total $ 530

* Printing Costs:
  - a. Business Cards (500) Thermographed to Foil Stamped from $19.95 to $89.00 — $ 55
  - b. Letterhead & Envelopes (500) from $130.00 to $187.00 basic stock — $ 140
  - c. Thank you notes (100) $34.00 to $89.00 — $ 50
  - d. Flyers (500) Black plus 1 stock color ink $69.00 to $129.00 — $ 100
  - e. Business Checks $15.00 to $27.00 — $ 20
  - f. Gift Basket Tags — $ 10

  Total $ 375

## Start-up Costs continued

*Advertising:
    a. Yellow Page Ad listed under
       **Gift-Baskets & Baskets-Retail**
       from $79.00 to $150.00 per month

$ _120_

Total $ _120_

* Deposits:
    a.  Business Insurance (Check with your
        Insurance agent)                          $ _____
    b.  Business Telephone (Check with your
        local telephone company.)                 $ _____
    c.  Others                                    $ _____

Total $ _____

* Beginning Inventory of Assorted Baskets:     $ _350 (can do for $200)_
* Gift Baskets Accessory Items:                $ _1,000 (can do for $500)_
* Basket Supplies:
    a. Hot Glue Gun                             $ _10_
    b. Excelsior, Straw, Woodfiber, or Paper Grass  $ _40 (enough for 50-60 baskets)_
    c. Silks, Dried Floral                      $ _100_
    d. Ribbon                                   $ _50_
    e. Cellophane                               $ _8 (2 rolls)_
    f. Hot Gun and Shrink Wrap                  $ _115_
       (optional)

Total $ _1,673_

* Fees
    a. Business License (Average $50.00)        $ _50_
    b. Fictitious Name Statement (Filing and
       Publication Cost...Average $50.00)       $ _50_
    c. Sellers Permit                           $ _____

Total $ _100_

* Misc.                                         $ _125_

Total $ _3,000_

## A Note About Visa and MasterCard Charges

USE YOUR
CREDIT CARD

Your business benefits substantially by being able to offer your customers Visa and MasterCard purchasing. However, it can be somewhat difficult for a home-based business to obtain a merchant bank card agreement with many of the banking institutions simply because they prefer dealing with storefront businesses. Also they need to know that your business sells enough product to warrant the use of a bank card merchant account. The growth of your business makes it worth the effort of finding a bank or other financial institution who will work with you.

## The Benefits of Being a Bank Card Merchant

* Customers look for convenience and ease of purchasing.

* Credit card purchasing can increase the average amount of your sales. Credit cards usually allow a customer to make a larger purchase than when using a personal check or cash.

* A customer will use a credit card when they do not have available cash, either on hand or in their checking account.

* To the merchant, all bank card sales are cash sales — no need to have funds tied up in receivables.

* All credit card transactions are credited to your business checking account the day they are deposited.

**Chapter 3**

# $T$HE BUSINESS OF BUSINESS

Now is your chance to become a corporation like IBM or Chrysler — or after talking to your accountant or lawyer, maybe a sole proprietorship or partnership.

## Sole Proprietorship

By definition, the term "sole proprietorship" means that a business is owned by a single person or entity (husband and wife) and is not incorporated. This type of business has been popular over the years because it is simple to set up and get started. It is the least regulated of all businesses, yet still offers all the opportunities to maintain your own control on how to run your business, make the decisions and keep the profits.

It is important to be aware of all the legal aspects of a sole proprietorship. As the sole proprietor, you are personally responsible for any debts or obligations incurred by the business. Damages from any lawsuits brought against the business can be taken from the personal assets of the owner.

An additional benefit of doing business as a sole proprietor is the avoidance of the double taxation which is encountered doing business as a corporation. The sole proprietorship is not considered a separate taxable entity from the operator, resulting in income being taxed only once to the operator. A financial professional can more fully explain the tax implications and consequences of doing business as a sole proprietor.

## Incorporation

The only way to avoid the unlimited personal liability of the sole proprietor is to incorporate. In general, the debts, obligations and legal liability of a corporation are limited to the assets of the business and are not the personal responsibility of the owner. Because we do not cover the definition of corporations in the book, we strongly advise that you consult with those knowledgeable in this field, such as an accountant or an attorney. From personal experience, we feel that a sole proprietorship is a good way to go for the Specialty Gift Basket Business. You cannot hire yourself as an employee, but you can withdraw any amount from the business to pay yourself. Just remember that this "draw" is not a wage and must be included on your personal income tax return.

One important factor in determining which form of business entity you wish to utilize is the additional burden of doing business as a corporation. As a tradeoff for allowing limited personal liabilities to the operator, the law requires additional filing, meeting and documentary formalities which must be adhered to. Failure to do so could result in the operators incurring personal liability. Again, we strongly advise consulting a knowledgeable professional regarding precisely what the requirements are.

## Partnership

When a husband and wife operate a business together, the business can be a corporation, a partnership, or a sole proprietorship. Each of these three legal forms of business requires different paperwork, varying cost of setup and each can result in differences in income, taxes, social security, and fringe benefits.

Partnerships differ from sole proprietorship because they can create more capital, more skills and ideas, plus the extra energy generated when two or more people are working together. Having a partner can mean relief from the pressures of doing everything yourself. With your partner overseeing the operation, there is no need to shut down the business when you go on vacation. But remember, in a partnership, individual partners can be held responsible for financial debts and legal obligations.

Like sole proprietors, partners cannot be employees of their partnerships. Partners share in the profits of the partnership.

# Selecting a Partner

**P**referably, choose a partner (even if a friend or relative) who shares the same areas of interest or at least compliments the business with special skills, so that you can provide and share useful, mutual assistance. Mutual respect of each other's values and judgment is important for productive interaction. You must be willing to meet formally and at regular intervals to keep the communication lines open if you don't work together on a daily basis.

As partners you will share your talents, business knowledge, and other expertise to help the business grow. This works well for many reasons. One is extremely talented in the creative sphere (the designing and creating of baskets), while the other has a knack for sales and marketing, taking charge of interfacing with the customer, building your client base, and taking care of the books. All of these factors prevent the problems of burnout and isolation. They also keep you fresh and competitive with today's ever-changing marketplace.

A partnership must have its own federal identification number, obtained by filing Form SS-4, "Employer's Federal Identification Number." If the partnership has no employees, note on the form that it is "FOR IDENTIFICATION ONLY." This will alert the IRS not to send you payroll forms.

Partnerships must file a partnership income tax return, although the partnership itself pays no taxes. Partnerships will need business licenses, seller's permits, and if operating under fictitious names, fictitious name statements.

Death or withdrawal of one partner or the addition of a new partner legally terminates a partnership. However, business can continue with a new partnership agreement.

## *Partnership Agreement*

A partnership agreement is an understanding and trust between partners as to how the business will be conducted. A written partnership agreement is not required by law, but it is something no partnership should be without. It reduces the possibilities of misunderstanding and future problems. Written partnership agreements should be signed by all the partners and should specify the following:

Describe the business and its goals. A simple, written statement of business goals is the first and most important step.

 The amount each partner will contribute — in cash, in property and in labor. There are no federal laws requiring partners to make equal or simultaneous contributions.

 How profits and losses will be divided among partners. The most common arrangement is an equal division of profits between partners.

 Provisions for continuing the business if one partner dies or wants out.

It is advisable to consult an attorney to draw up any partnership agreement. However, it is also possible to obtain a standardized Partnership Agreement form from your local stationery or office supply store. Just fill it out, have both partners sign it and have copies made for each of you. You might want to have an attorney or tax accountant look at it. Then file the document in a safe place.

PARTNERSHIP AGREEMENT

Dated

Commences

Expires

Location

# Licenses and Regulations

## Zoning

Check the zoning ordinances in your area. You need to be aware of them. If you don't have a high traffic business or disturb the neighbors there should be no problem. Generally speaking, zoning officials will check on home businesses only if someone is complaining, or there is an obvious violation. When it comes to zoning, be aware of some of the more common restrictions and ways to overcome them.

*"Always do right. This will surprise some people and astonish the rest."*
— Mark Twain

* **Space limitations** — There are usually space limitations imposed for business purposes (based on total residential square footage).

* **Foot traffic** — No continual business-related foot traffic.

To remedy this second point, it is a good idea to rent a private mailing address. A private post office provides you with a street address and a suite number instead of a box number. The cost is minimal on an annual basis. You can subscribe for a mailbox rental at your local postal annex service center and then all your catalogues, inventory, and business correspondence can be shipped there and held, rather than draw attention to deliveries at the home where neighbors might complain.

* **Signs** — Do not hang signs by your front walk in a residential area, nor display any signs in your window.

* **Noise** — Loud or unusual noises will certainly bring you to the attention of your neighbors.

* **Deliveries** — Make deliveries rather than have your customers pick up merchandise at your home if you are zoned residential. Pick up large orders of baskets or other inventory you have ordered so you do not disrupt the neighborhood with large delivery trucks.

*"I usually ordered most of our baskets from a supplier within 200 miles from where I lived. That way, I could do the pickup myself. This was beneficial in three ways: (1) I did not have to pay a freight charge for delivery (2) there was no disruption to my neighbors, and (3) it gave me a break from routine and kept me in personal touch with my suppliers."*
— Camille J. Anderson

* **Neighbor relations** — Build good neighbor relations. If they are supportive of your work, they can be your best "testimonial" should you need special permits or a variance to work at home.

* **Sales restrictions** — Adjust your business to meet any restrictions. If for example, retail sales are not permitted on your premises, distribute your products by delivering them or mail ordering advertising. You can call on your accounts with your brochure/portfolio displaying your basket line, place the order

and deliver your product to them. Once you create your clientele, phone orders are quite common.

Sometimes homeowners' and condominium association regulations include restrictions on using homes for business purposes. It is a good idea to find out what these are before setting up, and if there is a restriction, how it might be handled in an alternate way.

*"Our neighbors never complained as the gift baskets were a welcome diversion."*

Camille J. Anderson

## DBA — Fictitious Name Statement

When a business goes by any name other than the owner's real name, the business is being operated under a fictitious name (also known as an "assumed name" or a "DBA", doing business as). You must file a DBA with the county in which you will conduct your business. The county will charge a filing fee of about $10.00. Filing a DBA or Fictitious Name Statement prevents any other business in the county from using the same business name.

In addition to filing for a fictitious name, you will be required to publish the Fictitious Name Statement in a newspaper "of general circulation" in the area. The ad usually has to run four consecutive issues. The theory behind this is that the public has a right to know with whom they are doing business. The county clerk in your area can provide you with a list of acceptable newspapers. Publication costs are relatively low if your county has a newspaper that specializes in running legal notices. If not, small-time newspapers almost always charge less than large-circulation dailies.

You will be required to renew your fictitious name periodically, usually once every five years. In many states, the county notifies you when your renewal is due. If you forget to renew, someone else can step in and file for your business name, and you will not be able to use it any more.

## Local Business Licenses

As a business owner, you must have a local business license (either city or county, depending on where you operate). These licenses can be obtained at the local city hall or county offices.

## Sales and Use Taxes

With a limited number of exceptions, every business that sells tangible personal property to customers must obtain a seller's permit (also called "resale numbers" or "resale permits") from the State Board of Equalization office nearest your place of business. Oregon doesn't have a sales tax, so of course, if you live there, you don't have to worry about sales tax. In most states, you will have to go down to your local Board of Equalization office and register in person, since they will not process mailed-in applications. There is no fee for obtaining a seller's permit; however, you might be required to post a bond as security for payment of tax.

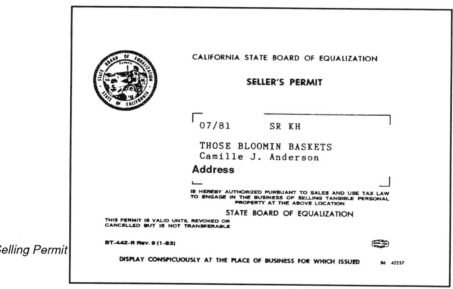

CALIFORNIA STATE BOARD OF EQUALIZATION

**SELLER'S PERMIT**

07/81      SR KH

THOSE BLOOMIN BASKETS
Camille J. Anderson
**Address**

IS HEREBY AUTHORIZED PURSUANT TO SALES AND USE TAX LAW TO ENGAGE IN THE BUSINESS OF SELLING TANGIBLE PERSONAL PROPERTY AT THE ABOVE LOCATION
STATE BOARD OF EQUALIZATION
THIS PERMIT IS VALID UNTIL REVOKED OR CANCELLED BUT IS NOT TRANSFERABLE

BT-442-R Rev. 9 (1-83)

DISPLAY CONSPICUOUSLY AT THE PLACE OF BUSINESS FOR WHICH ISSUED      84  47257

*Selling Permit*

As a retailer, you must collect and pay the state a certain percentage of sales tax (depending upon your location) on all taxable sales. However, if you are selling at wholesale (selling to a retailer), you will not collect sales tax on goods you sell if the retailer (or wholesaler) holds a valid seller's permit and provides you his "resale certificate."

Likewise, when you operate as a retailer or wholesaler, you may buy goods (merchandise) for resale and you don't pay sales tax to the wholesalers if you provide them with your resale permit. Once you register your resale permit with each wholesaler or manufacturer, you need not fill out this form every time you purchase unless it expires (most suppliers update their files once a year). You cannot use your seller's permit to make tax-free purchases of office supplies, tools, or equipment, or any product to be used for personal, non-business purposes. By definition, wholesale refers to a sale of goods by one business to another for resale or manufacture.

In those states that have a sales tax, the sales and use tax laws require a business that sells tangible personal property to keep complete records of the gross receipts from sales. You must also keep complete records, including tax returns, to substantiate all deductions claimed on sales and of the total purchase price of all tangible personal property bought for resale in most states.

Sales and tax returns usually must be filed and tax paid within one month after the end of each calendar quarter (or year) depending upon the size and income of your business.

## Federal Identification Numbers

Your gift basket business must be identified on tax forms and licenses by either one of two numbers.

*"... your Social Security number or a Federal Employer Identification Number." A Social Security number is all the identification needed by a sole proprietorship until you hire employees. Then, you will have to get the Federal Employer ID Number. To get an ID number, file Form SS-4 with the IRS. No fee is charged. If you do file for and receive a Federal Employer Identification Number, the IRS will automatically send you quarterly and year-end payroll tax returns that you must fill out and return even if you have no employees. So don't apply for an Employer ID Number until you become an employer."*

*"Partnerships and corporations must have federal and/or state identification numbers whether they hire employees or not."*
— Bernard Kamoroff, *Small-Time Operator*

## Federal Trade Commission Rules

If you make any statement or product guarantees and warranties, you must use specific wording according to the Consumer Products Warranty Law.

Mail order businesses must comply with a Federal Trade Commission rule designed to crack down on undue mail order shipping delays.

Current information on all Federal Trade Commission regulations is available from the FTC, Washington, D.C. 20580. These FTC regulations are constantly changing.

For the purposes of running a gift-filled, specialty basket business out of the home, there are no other permits or licenses that you will need. However, it is still advisable to check with your local governmental agencies to make sure. If you decide to get into exporting your baskets to foreign countries, you will be required to fill out forms and apply for licenses. If you are importing goods into the United States, you should acquaint yourself with customs procedures, shipping costs and custom duties. The U.S. Customs Service publishes a booklet entitled Importing Into the U.S., available from the U.S. Government Printing Office, Washington D.C. 20402.

## Liquor Laws

Concerning beer, wine, champagne or any other alcoholic beverage used for decorating a basket: liquor laws differ in all states and we strongly recommend that you stay in compliance with all state and federal laws. For example, the State of California will issue a beer and wine license to qualified retail outlets. However, it will not issue a license to someone working from their home. Check with your state's Alcohol Beverage Control Board for their rules and regulations.

## Child labor Laws

Just to be on the safe side and in case you will use your children or young relatives to help you in your business, check on the child labor laws in your state.

# Business Insurance

**P**repare for that unexpected rainy day. It is important to investigate your insurance needs based on how you are set up in your home.

The rule of thumb is that business property cannot be included with personal property on your home policy. Check with your agent and he or she will advise you based on your own personal situation.

A variety of insurance coverage is available. Contact the state you live in, your bank if you plan to get a loan, or your insurance agent before you make any decisions on insurance.

☐ **Business Property Insurance** — Your basic homeowner's or apartment dweller's insurance policy covers damage or loss only to your personal property. It may have restrictions on coverage for business use of your home. Call an agent and inquire about the limits and restrictions on your policy to insure that you have enough coverage for any damage or loss to your business property. In most situations, if you purchase special coverage for business and personal property and also liability and medical expense, it should be ample to also cover the business. Since the agent's fee tends to increase with greater insurance coverage, you could end up paying more than you need to. Find an agent that is knowledgeable, reliable, and someone you can trust. As a start, ask friends, lawyers, accountants, and other professionals to recommend a good insurance agent.

☐ **Health Insurance** — If you are self-employed or working at another job and your employer does not have health insurance, then you need to find an affordable plan. Shop around. Health insurance can be purchased individually or as a part of a group policy. There are many options available when covered under a group plan. There are even plans available to gift basket retailers. Some insurance agents specialize in placing small businesses in "multiple employer trusts." The first option to look at is the possibility of getting coverage under a company policy of an employed spouse.

☐ **Automobile Insurance** — Check with your agent to see how to obtain coverage that includes the business use of your automobile.

☐ **Products Liability Insurance** — This protects you in case your products cause injury to the user. In manufacturing a product from home, one has to be extremely cautious, especially when dealing with food items because of spoilage. Any product that is defective or unsafe when used is a liability to the manufacturer or seller. Be well informed about this law and investigate this insurance to protect yourself.

When and if you decide to expand or move and open a retail store, check with your insurance agent for further details on coverage.

| | |
|---|---|
| » Basic Fire Insurance | » Extended Coverage |
| » Liability Insurance | » Vandalism Insurance |
| » Business Interruption | » Workers' Compensation Insurance |

## Checklist for Starting Out

The stage is set for you to make your first sale, except for one last detail — a business license. Depending on the nature of the business and on state and local government regulations in your area you might need to obtain a local business license.

☐ Register your business name (file a Fictitious Name Statement DBA)

☐ Obtain a Seller's Permit, Resale Certificate of Authority for sales-tax purposes.

☐ Have an Employer's I.D. Number (Use Form SS-4)

☐ Obtain federal or state licenses (if required)

☐ Partnerships: File a statement of partnership

☐ Corporations: File articles of incorporation.

**Chapter 4**

# SETTING UP A BOOK-KEEPING SYSTEM

*"I don't know how much money I've got. I did ask the accountant how much it came to. I wrote it down on a bit of paper but I've lost the bit of paper."*
— John Lennon

Setting up a good bookkeeping system is an important part of every business. Your books are the only source of complete and comprehensive information about your business. It is crucial that you do not mix your business expenses with personal expenses. It causes confusion and trauma if you need to validate your records for the IRS. Many business failures have been blamed on the lack of accurate financial records. So, be survivors and keep good records for your Specialty Gift Basket Business.

*"Business failures have been blamed time and time again on a lack of financial records."*
— Bernard Kamoroff

There are many systems to choose from in the marketplace. The system most accountants and CPAs recommend is commonly referred to as the pegboard system. It is a complete record keeping system and is ideal for a growing business. It employs an excellent method for organizing your check writing and bookkeeping into one. Essential information is duplicated directly onto journal sheets as you write out your checks, thereby saving time. It allows you to minimize your effort and maximize your organization. Multiple records are integrated into one easy method that improves accuracy and virtually eliminates bookkeeping errors. Check with your bank for information on how to obtain this type of system.

Keep your bookkeeping system very simple. Starting out in your own business as a one person operator doesn't require an elaborate or complicated bookkeeping system. If you find that the pegboard type system is not for you, choose a simple single-entry system ultilizing both a cash receipt ledger and a cash disbursement ledger that can be found at any stationery store. A cash receipt ledger records income and sales tax. A cash disbursement ledger records all expenses for your business. You might even decide that you would rather pay someone who is an expert in accounting to keep your books for you. A few important factors worthy of your consideration are highlighted here.

1. As we have already mentioned, you need to open a business checking account with your business name and address.

2. Pay all your business bills by check because this gives you better documentation on your expenses.

3. Keep canceled checks and/or expense receipts in separate envelopes. At the end of the month, staple the receipts to your canceled checks and place them in an accordion file by categories. Also, record all expenses onto your cash disbursement ledger monthly.

4. In your accordion file, you should have the following individual sections to file monthly paper work. Create labels for each section:

    (a) Advertising Expense (cost of photo processing, printing for brochures, etc. and any other expense to promote your baskets)

    (b) Automobile Expense (separate envelope for gasoline, car repair, maintenance, insurance, parking and tolls)

    (c) Inventory Purchases (baskets and basket supplies)

    (d) Office Supply Expense

    (e) Postage

    (f) Telephone Expense

(g) Entertainment and Travel Expense

(h) Miscellaneous Expense

5. Deposit all checks and cash from business income into your business bank account.

6. It is imperative to balance your bank account every month. Keep all your bank statements and canceled checks for a minimum of three years. It is now common practice for banks to use electronic files and not return your canceled checks, but you will receive a monthly statement with your checks listed by number and amount.

7. Follow two steps when recording income:

(a) At the time a sale is made, record that sale on an appropriate invoice, cash receipt or cash register receipt.

(b) Summarize the sales in a cash receipt journal.

When you start out, it is fine to use the preprinted cash receipts (found in any stationery or volume discount store). As your clientele builds, you can have invoices printed (custom-designed forms), with your business name and logo. This gives a more professional appearance, especially when working with businesses and corporations.

8. Whether you use a prenumbered receipt book, or custom invoices, the forms should be in duplicate — one for your customer and one for your records. On these forms you must show the name of your business, address and telephone; date of sale; customer's name and address; description of sale; amount showing sales tax and shipping charges separately (if appropriate); and a space to indicate when paid. The duplicate copies that you keep will later be summarized and transferred to your cash receipt journal. If you void an invoice, do not discard it. Mark the invoice "VOID" and keep it in your receipt book.

9. The cash receipt journal is kept to record your sales and invoices, whether they are handwritten or from a cash register. The journal summarizes exactly how much you have sold on a monthly or yearly basis. This journal helps you project your slow and busy months in order to create a flow chart and it will provide financial information for Sales and Use Tax Reports and income taxes.

10. To start out, you might want to transfer all your sales and sales tax information onto your receipt journal only once a month. Keep all your sales receipts, expenditures, etc. in separate folders or envelopes.

11. Segregate business loans and personal contributions to your business account from your normal cash receipts of the business as they are nontaxable receipts.

12. Do not use the business account to pay personal or nonbusiness expenses. You can, however, make a withdrawal or personal draw by writing a check payable to yourself or payable to cash.

13. Keep a mileage record for each month — beginning mileage for the month, ending mileage, miles used for business, and personal mileage. This way you have an ongoing record and will not have to spend hours at the end of the year calculating mileage for income tax purposes. Develop a method that works best for you. Whatever works — use it!

14. If you have expenses that are partly personal and partly business, such as automobile, rent or utilities, they should be paid from your personal bank account. Have your accountant help you with this.

## MILEAGE LOG

| Month Date | Purpose of Trip Person/Reason | Odometer Start | End | Total Miles | Gas, Repairs, etc. Cost -Description |
|---|---|---|---|---|---|
| | | | | | |
| | | | | | |
| | | | | | |
| | | | | | |
| | | | | | |
| | | | | | |
| | | | | | |
| | | | | | |
| | | | | | |
| | | | | | |

If you rent a business premises separate from your home, post the full amount of the rent to that column. However, if you are using a portion of your home for your shop or office, you must follow a different procedure. First determine whether or not you are allowed a deduction for office or shop in your home. *The IRS tax laws change constantly and you must check this or ask your accountant.*

If you are eligible for a home/office deduction and if you own or are buying your home, you cannot deduct all expenses. You can depreciate only a portion of the cost of your home as a business expense. Depreciation should be calculated once a year, at year-end. If you rent your home (and you qualify for the deduction), you must determine what percentage of your home is used for business. As mentioned before, under IRS rules, the percentage is based on the amount of space devoted to business. Always check with your accountant.

## If You Have a Computer

There are various software programs available on the market that enable you to do basic accounting and bookkeeping on your computer. They range from the very simple systems for personal financial needs for the Specialty Gift Basket Business, all the way to a highly sophisticated system for large organizations. There are many features in each software program. Some of these include:

- Accounts payable ledger

- General ledger

- Payroll

- Expenditure ledger

- Program for maintaining accounts payable and receivable

- Program for tracking orders

- Program to track cash flow

- Program for preparing bills

- Program to prepare sales tax reports

- Program for monitoring project costs

- Program to calculate federal and state taxes

- Program for inventory tracking

You can purchase basic software programs for under $200 that include a general ledger, accounts payable, and accounts receivable. Expansion modules are available for customizing reports and invoices.

There are many sources for locating the software program that you will need, including: computer stores, software stores, software services and directories, mail order, consultants, or user groups.

## Extending Credit

It is not a good idea to extend credit to your customers (this is not to be confused with the use of credit cards for payments). Credit selling involves much more work and bookkeeping and headaches! You do not want to be bothered with trying to collect past-due accounts from slow or nonpaying customers. Deal in direct terms — 100% down and no monthly payments! This rule may be waived, at your discretion, when working with businesses or corporations that place a large order. With large orders, ask for a 50% down payment, and the remainder within 30 days. Another way is to ask for your 50% down to start the order and the remainder paid on delivery of the order.

# Chapter 5

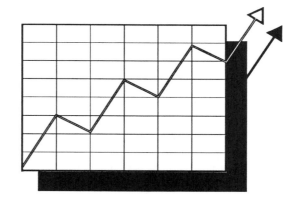

# PERSONAL GOALS — BUSINESS GOALS

**P**erhaps you selected the SPECIALTY GIFT BASKET BUSINESS because of certain skills you possess. Or you thought that it would be a fun and enjoyable way to make money and give you the independence you have been striving for. Whatever the reason, getting the most out of your business will require that you take constructive action that leads to worthwhile results.

One way for you to identify your objectives is to answer the questions of WHY, WHAT, WHEN, WHERE, HOW, and WHO in the form of a statement:

---

I/we (WHO) _Mary Jones and Jean Carter_ have opened a (WHAT) _Specialty Gift Basket Business_ in (WHERE)_West Hills, CA_ on (WHEN) _Date_ (WHY) _so that I/We can have the challenge to capitalize on all of my/our creative abilities, independence to manage my/our own decisions, and, most important to have financial freedom._ This will be accomplished (HOW) _by constantly educating myself/ourselves and learning about and applying new marketing and selling technologies._ I/We _will plan a program of constructive action for success in obtaining my/our personal and business income goals._

---

# Plan of Action for Staying on Target

**M**anaging the different roles you'll play in your business requires a plan and then following the plan with action. It is difficult for you to attain any degree of success without knowing where you are going, how much money your business can bring in to start, how profitable it can become, and how to best spend your time to achieve your goals. To organize all the activities in your business — creating and assembling the baskets; delivering the baskets; selling, marketing, and customer service; ordering inventory; attending gift and gourmet food shows — all of these require a great deal of time management discipline and short term and long term planning for sales and business development.

*"Any business must always plan ahead, either to capitalize on success or to reverse the trend if not successful."*

—Anonymous

This portion of the book lays an easy-to-follow path resulting in a highly professional approach to successful selling techniques and business development. Each major section contains instructions, examples of practical forms, and worksheets in a natural progression for developing you and your Specialty Gift Basket Business.

## *Specialty Gift Basket Business Plan*

Once you decide to be in the Specialty Gift Basket Business, you need to write out a basic business plan. The following sample business plan outline can help you get your business up and running.

---

### SAMPLE BUSINESS PLAN

**1. Your company name**_____

**2. Name of owner(s)**. A legal contract to determine the shared ownership of the business._____

---

**3. Management responsibility**. If a partnership is formed, who is the key decision maker? Who is accountable and responsible for running the business? How much time is each partner to spend on the business?

_____

_____

_____

_____

**4. Financial sources** — Where will start-up money come from? If a partnership is formed what are the cash contributions from all partners? Detail the way the money will be invested into the business. How will the profit be split? Create a legal partnership agreement (you may want to consult an attorney)._____

_____

_____

_____

_____

_____

**5. Future growth of the business.** State your specific short term (one-year) goals, and state specific long term (two-, three-, four- to five-year) goals. Anticipate and detail buy out agreements, expansion plans and the sale of the business._____

_____

_____

_____

_____

_____

**6. Business location**. Where will the business be located and under what conditions? Will the location be suitable for walk-in traffic if you have a home based operation—are you in compliance with the zoning regulations? Will you have a retail store?_____

_____

_____

_____

_____

**7. Market strategy**. Describe your plan of action for marketing such as word-of-mouth, direct mail advertising, newspaper advertising, advertising in local Yellow Pages, direct sales to the corporate market, church newsletter, and so on._____

_____

_____

_____

_____

**8. Identify the competition**. What are their strengths and weaknesses?_____

_____

_____

_____

**9. Economic projections.** State and write out exactly how this business will make money._____

_____

_____

_____

_____

# Income Needs and Wants

Defining your income *needs* is one thing, but obtaining your business income goals to meet your personal income *wants* is another thing. This section will help you to define your income *needs* as well as what you *want*.

Set up a business budget to distinguish between personal income and business income needs. Whether or not the gift basket business is going to subsidize your income or be your primary source of income, we suggest you take the approach described in the following paragraphs.

To determine your income needs, figure out exactly what will be required to produce your projected cash flow for a twelve-month period. The budget must cover both personal and business expenditures.

After you have projected and arrived at your *basic* income *requirements*, it is time to project your *idealistic* income *wants*. The basic goal of your business is to set a realistic budget for earning the money necessary to meet basic financial needs in accordance with your present standard of living. Your business budget will take into account inventory, advertising, marketing, auto expenses, taxes, insurance, telephone and utilities, entertainment, travel, and last but not least, your salary draw to meet your personal standard of living.

The easiest and best way to determine your basic financial needs is to analyze how you spent your money last year. Go back through your canceled checks, receipts, and any other records that reflect how your money was spent in accordance with your existing income. If your basket business is going to be located in your home make certain that there isn't a duplication of expenses on your personal budget that might be on your business budget, like rent or mortgage payments.

# Preparing a Realistic Budget

The accurate evaluation of last year's expenses is the most realistic guideline to use in preparing your budget. This keeps you on track for developing and preparing a realistic budget to calculate your expected expenses for the next year, remembering that you'll want to factor in allowances for price increases, inflation, and any exceptional or unexpected expenses.

Because the gift basket business, for the most part, revolves around peak holiday seasons, you will see a variable income. At Christmas, Valentine's Day and other major holidays, you will earn in excess of your budgetary requirements. When you find yourself with extra money, it is wise to invest a large portion of it back into the business for inventory, advertising, or maybe equipment upgrades. Try to avoid the temptation to spend the money on personal extras, especially in the early development stage. Live within your personal budget until the business has grown substantially, before you expand your personal standard of living.

To help you develop your personal budget, we show examples of budget sheets — one for last year's actual expenses, and one to project this year's personal budget plan. The sample forms list the general categories of expenses that you can use to create your own budget plans by adding categories pertinent to your situation.

## ACTUAL EXPENSES FROM LAST YEAR

| | JANUARY | FEBRUARY | MARCH | APRIL | MAY |
|---|---|---|---|---|---|
| Rent or Mortgage Payments | | | | | |
| Disability Insurance | | | | | |
| Fire and General Insurance | | | | | |
| Income and State Tax | | | | | |
| Property Taxes | | | | | |
| Social Security Taxes | | | | | |
| | | | | | |
| Food | | | | | |
| Clothing and Footwear | | | | | |
| Laundry and Tailoring | | | | | |
| Non-business Lunches | | | | | |
| Maintenance of Home and Yard | | | | | |
| Furniture and Appliances | | | | | |
| | | | | | |
| Automobile Payment | | | | | |
| Auto Maintenance | | | | | |
| Gasoline | | | | | |
| Insurance | | | | | |
| | | | | | |
| Electricity | | | | | |
| Natural Gas | | | | | |
| Oil | | | | | |
| Water | | | | | |
| Telephone | | | | | |
| | | | | | |
| Health, Accident, Hospitalization Ins. | | | | | |
| Doctor | | | | | |
| Dentist | | | | | |
| Medical Needs, Prescriptions | | | | | |
| | | | | | |
| Savings Account | | | | | |
| Life Insurance | | | | | |
| Investments | | | | | |
| Debt Reduction | | | | | |
| | | | | | |
| Charitable Donations | | | | | |
| Entertainment and Vacation | | | | | |
| Clubs and Lodge Dues | | | | | |
| Gifts and Services | | | | | |

## THIS YEAR'S "BUDGET" PLAN

| | JANUARY | FEBRUARY | MARCH | APRIL | MAY |
|---|---|---|---|---|---|
| Rent or Mortgage Payments | | | | | |
| Disability Insurance | | | | | |
| Fire and General Insurance | | | | | |
| Income and State Tax | | | | | |
| Property Taxes | | | | | |
| Social Security Taxes | | | | | |
| | | | | | |
| Food | | | | | |
| Clothing and Footwear | | | | | |
| Laundry and Tailoring | | | | | |
| Non-business Lunches | | | | | |
| Maintenance of Home and Yard | | | | | |
| Furniture and Appliances | | | | | |
| | | | | | |
| Automobile Payment | | | | | |
| Auto Maintenance | | | | | |
| Gasoline | | | | | |
| Insurance | | | | | |
| | | | | | |
| Electricity | | | | | |
| Natural Gas | | | | | |
| Oil | | | | | |
| Water | | | | | |
| Telephone | | | | | |
| | | | | | |
| Health, Accident, Hospitalization Ins. | | | | | |
| Doctor | | | | | |
| Dentist | | | | | |
| Medical Needs, Prescriptions | | | | | |
| | | | | | |
| Savings Account | | | | | |
| Life Insurance | | | | | |
| Investments | | | | | |
| Debt Reduction | | | | | |
| | | | | | |
| Charitable Donations | | | | | |
| Entertainment and Vacation | | | | | |
| Clubs and Lodge Dues | | | | | |
| Gifts and Services | | | | | |

| JUNE | JULY | AUGUST | SEPTEMBER | OCTOBER | NOVEMBER | DECEMBER | TOTAL |
|------|------|--------|-----------|---------|----------|----------|-------|
|      |      |        |           |         |          |          |       |
|      |      |        |           |         |          |          |       |
|      |      |        |           |         |          |          |       |
|      |      |        |           |         |          |          |       |

*Planning-Ahead Sheet*

# Daily Work Plans and Activities

**M**ake every day a *creative* workday. Work can be fun if you figure out in advance what you need to accomplish to reach your goals.

*"To business that we love, we rise betimes and go to it with delight."*
— William Shakespeare

Daily work plans and activities will flow over into weekly and then into monthly work plans; the result is that you'll find that by working smarter, the work will be easier.

It is important for you to plan how much of your daily activities are directed toward selling. Sales will make up a large part of your workday; therefore it is necessary and valuable for you to keep track of how much you earn on each sales call or contact. The work activity example below is designed primarily to help formulate and measure your daily efforts and direct them in the most profitable way and to keep on track with your income goals.

## *Figuring Your Work Activities...*

Adapt the following table using your projected income and use it to figure out your daily, weekly, and monthly work activities to meet these income needs and goals.

**Line 1.** Enter the total income needed from your business and your desired income goals.

**Line 2.** Enter your average gross profit per sale under the Need column and under the Goals column.

**Line 3.** Enter your Total Number of Sales Needed. This is arrived at by dividing your average gross profit per sale (Line 2) into Total Income (Line 1).

### MONTHLY INCOME PLAN & WORK ACTIVITIES FORM

|  |  | NEEDS (REQUIRED) | GOALS ( DESIRES) |
|---|---|---|---|
| Line 1 | Total Income | $4,000.00 | $5,000.00 |
| Line 2 | Average gross profit per order | 250.00 | 250.00 |
| Line 3 | Total number of sales needed | 16 | 20 |
|  |  |  |  |

Of course, you can expand on this concept. If your best and most profitable marketing efforts are through home parties, do a separate table for this category to compare the percentage of business generated from home parties to other marketing efforts such as corporate accounts, advertising in the Yellow Pages, fairs, swap meets, flea markets, etc. There may be additional areas that you will need feedback on such as how many phone calls it took to set an appointment, or how many appointments to make one sale. Another area might be how many fliers were passed out to offices to generate a presentation, and how many presentations resulted in how many sales.

# Keep Score to Stay on Track

**I**t has been said that one must grow like a tree, not like a mushroom. In the business world today a personal development plan must be ongoing and flexible. *"The business graveyard is filled with companies that failed to consider and plan for inevitable changes."* When we fail to make changes in our personal development, it is often reflected in our businesses.

Capitalize on existing behavior and personality strengths and continue to build on them. Recognize your weaker areas and develop them into strengths or turn them over to someone who is better equipped and willing to handle them.

What you do today will determine the future existence of your business tomorrow. A compilation of your daily results will help you stay on track and keep you committed to reaching your goals. This perhaps, in the beginning, may appear cumbersome, but it takes only a few minutes a day to accomplish. The results of maintaining a record of your daily activities will enable you, at a glance, to see if you are ahead, behind, or on schedule.

A simple method for keeping score is to always carry a small 3x5-card with you to record the following activities:

| Name | M | T | W | T | F | S | Total |
|---|---|---|---|---|---|---|---|
| # of appointments | | | | | | | |
| # of contacts | | | | | | | |
| # of presentations | | | | | | | |
| # of sales | | | | | | | |
| # of new leads | | | | | | | |

**My income goals for the week of** ___/___/___ **$**_____
**My actual income for the week of** ___/___/___ **$**_____

Do the same with your advertising:

Cost of Advertisement _ _ _ _ _ _ _
Number of responses  _ _ _ _ _ _ _
Number of Sales _ _ _ _ _ _ _ _ _
Comments  _ _ _ _ _ _ _ _ _ _ _

_ _ _ _ _ _ _ _ _ _ _ _ _ _ _ _

Keep track of the number of responses from the Yellow Pages, the newspapers, and fliers or brochures that are delivered around the neighborhood and business community. When you get phone calls inquiring about your baskets, remember to ask the party how they heard about you. This is very important as it will let you know if you are spending your advertising dollars on the right media.

From your daily activity card, compile a weekly and then a monthly record. This will also assist you in reevaluating and resetting your goals.

# Your Personal Development Plan

*"More creativity is the only way to make tomorrow better than today."*
— Anonymous

Though it may be a myth to assume that there is a certain type of "business personality," it is true that successful business people build on their personal strengths at the same time they work to develop other desirable traits of character and personality.

Successful and creative business people have a propensity toward knowing and utilizing the strengths they already have to their best advantage. At the same time, they employ the means necessary to improve their weaker personality traits.

As you build your business, you'll find new and resourceful ways to accomplish things that you didn't think possible. However, you'll be challenged in areas where you have no experience, and may have a tendency to have less confidence in carrying out a task at hand. Lack of confidence has a way of sabotaging the very thing we want to accomplish.

Webster defines confidence as, "firm belief; trust; belief in one's own abilities; reliance on one's own powers (the confidence that you will win)." Confidence can usually be associated with experience and growth, as an old Chinese proverb says, "Be not afraid of growing slowly, be afraid only of standing still." The success of your business will depend on, among other factors, the confidence you possess and the manner in which you present yourself and your company.

Start off on the right foot. Always dress professionally to make a sales presentation. Before entering a home or office, take a deep breath, pull those slumped shoulders back and visualize your client enjoying your beautiful baskets.

Know the purpose of your call. Is it a cold call to cultivate future business, or centers of influence? Is it a call-back to a corporate account? Is it a delivery of a basket to a client? Always be prepared with handouts. Leave behind brochures, order forms, and business cards.

Building and developing confidence in the beginning of your basket business can be a simple task if you apply a few strategies:

➤ Believe in yourself and what you have to offer.

➤ Be prepared in your approach and presentation to a prospective client.

➤ Know that we all have different opinions, and not everyone will share yours.

➤ Know that feedback from others, negative or positive, can be a learning tool to help improve your business.

➤ When your results for the day are down and you feel like giving up, remember this:

*"Good timber does not grow with ease, the stronger the wind the stronger the trees."*

— J. Willard Marriott

Having a personal development plan can and should be an on-going, simultaneous activity along with the development of your business. As a business person, you will begin to recognize those areas that need further development and take immediate actions to remedy the situation. The following ideas will help you in setting a strategy for building on your major strengths and working on areas that need improvement.

1. On one sheet of paper list all your major strengths that you will build on. On another sheet list all the areas that you need to develop and work on.

2. Next find out where to obtain source material that will teach you to develop whatever areas that need working on.

## Develop Sales Skills

*"He who has a thing to sell and goes and whispers in a well, is not so apt to get the dollars as he who climbs a tree and hollers."*

— Anonymous

The steps to take for a successful sale are divided into easy-to-understand segments that will help you develop better skills. You'll find these segments much easier to refer back to when you run into difficulties with selling techniques or you experience a sales slump in your business.

1. Prospecting for clients and suggested ideas on how to keep clients knocking down your doors for your baskets.

2. Having a well thought-out presentation, plus ideas and formulas for finding out what your clients' needs are and sell to those needs.

3. Identifying sales slumps and how to pull yourself out of them.

4. Time Management — setting priorities for your daily activities.

Sales skills can be best described as the actions you employ to make a sale, such as:

➤ Prospecting for clients to whom you'll sell your products and services

➤ Planning and giving your presentation

➤ Handling any clients' objections i.e., "Your price is too high."

➤ Telephoning for appointments

➤ Closing the sale

➤ Developing good time management skills

➤ Developing good communications and sales techniques.

All of the above skills must be developed, and continually improved upon through a goal-setting action program. To help you do this, we have provided a checklist that if answered truthfully, can quickly pinpoint any of your sales skills that need improvement. You can tackle the problem you encounter with confidence and commitment to overcome any obstacle that seems to be in your way. With this process, it becomes almost impossible for you to try to fake it or deceive yourself as to what must be corrected. Self-deception rates high among the causes of failure in business. So shape up and don't deceive yourself.

## Sales Problem Daily Checklist

Here is the checklist to give you a quick, simple way to check yourself, diagnose any sales problems and keep you constantly improving all your techniques. Take the liberty to change the numbers or items to represent what you need to be successful.

| | YES | NO |
|---|---|---|
| **1. PROSPECTING** | | |
| **a)** Are you securing a minimum of fifteen prospects? | ____ | ____ |
| **b)** Are you developing centers of influence? | ____ | ____ |
| **c)** Are you getting a minimum of six referrals on home parties? | ____ | ____ |
| **d)** Are you getting a minimum of six referrals on every sale? | ____ | ____ |
| **e)** Are you sending out twenty five brochures to companies? | ____ | ____ |
| **2. APPOINTMENTS** | | |
| **a)** Do you have five appointments each day to make a presentation? | ____ | ____ |
| **b)** Are you organizing your prospects to call the next morning? | ____ | ____ |
| **c)** Do you follow up on canceled appointments? | ____ | ____ |

### 3. PRESENTATIONS

**a)** Do you have a minimum of five face-to-face presentations today? _____ _____

**b)** Did you have a minimum of five face-to-face presentations yesterday? _____ _____

**c)** Do you have a minimum of one house party this week? _____ _____

### 4. TIME MANAGEMENT

**a)** Each night, do you prepare an "A" - and "B" - priority list? _____ _____

**b)** Do you allow time to prepare your baskets for the next day delivery? _____ _____

**c)** Do you schedule personal time for yourself and family? _____ _____

**d)** Do you schedule time for reading about new ideas? _____ _____

**e)** Have you scheduled lunch with a new client or center of influence? _____ _____

### 5. ATTITUDE

**a)** Do you work on personal development daily? _____ _____

**b)** Do you see positive results daily? _____ _____

**c)** Do you listen to motivational and business tapes in your car? _____ _____

---

*"In many businesses, today will end at five o'clock. Those bent on success, however, make today last from yesterday right through to tomorrow."*
— Lawrence H. Martin

## The Process-of-Elimination Approach

In addition to the checklist, you can take the process-of-elimination approach to identify sales problems. For instance, your business is going through a sales slump and you are seeing lower sales than normal. The problem can be identified through the following question and answer process. Read through the example so that you will understand the process:

Your gift basket business is conducted from your home. Your customer base is generated by Yellow Page advertising and calling on corporations and businesses. Your problem is low sales. Ask yourself if it is possible that you are making too few presentations. Is it because you are not closing the sales properly (letting the customer get away)? If your answer is "Yes, I am not making enough presentations" — ask yourself WHY! Is it because you are reluctant to make the calls or do you have difficulty setting up a presentation appointment after you have the customer on the line? If your answer is that you have plenty of prospects and don't mind making the calls, then it is narrowed down to your sales technique over the phone. If that is the case, you can now concentrate on improving your telephone-sales technique.

This is a simple method for identifying sales problems. The concept can be expanded to improve time management and the effectiveness of your marketing approach. For example, if you do a considerable amount of advertising in local newspapers and receive few or no sales, it could be due to low circulation, poor ad copy, or it might not be reaching your market. Just follow the same problem-solving concept and correct the problem.

*"No one can succeed unless he is willing to give his best--and nothing but his best."*

— Anonymous

# EFFECTIVE TIME MANAGEMENT

In this business, as in any small business, you'll have to wear many hats, and handle varying tasks each day which will present a challenge in how to accomplish everything in a minimum amount of time. Your income will be directly affected by how efficiently you handle all your tasks within the usual workday

There will be a tendency on your part to spend time on whatever facet of the business is most exciting to you, while neglecting to attend to other areas that are equally important to the growth and success of your business. It is essential to take an inventory of how your time is spent, and what each task you perform is worth in monetary value. This should be done from the beginning and continued on a regular basis.

For example, you received an order to do 100 centerpieces for one of your clients, and each centerpiece had a profit of $10.00. The time you allocated to construct the centerpieces and deliver them to your client involved about 14 hours. Divide the $1000.00 by 14 hours and you find that you made $71.43 as your hourly gross profit.

Now, let's assume that every face-to-face presentation you make results in an average sale of $75.00, and you make three face-to-face presentations every day which take a total of four hours. That's 3x $75.00 equaling $225.00 per day or $56.25 per hour. These examples give you a reference point for comparison so that you can put a value on time for any given task and maintain good time management.

*"Most misfortunes are the result of misused time."*
— Napoleon Hill

Time is perhaps our most precious commodity. Time can neither be recaptured nor suspended for later use. Therefore the tasks we have to accomplish must be managed within the time available to each one of us and we all have the same supply of time.

Nothing in the world, no magic formula, no miracle can provide you with additional time. However, effective time management will produce multiple benefits making better use of the time you now waste. Procrastination is one of the biggest thieves of time. When you stop procrastinating and gain increased control of your use of time, you begin to accomplish in one day the amount of work you stretched over a period of two to three days.

Benjamin Franklin said, "Time is money." Time is a resource that is available to all of us — to utilize in achieving our goals in life. However, it is a resource that can be misused, so we must take the responsibility of control over that resource. When you begin to feel stressed over not having time available to complete all the many demands of your business or home life, stop and study how you are spending your time. How many times did the phone ring and the calling party want a "quick" answer to a question and the conversation became an exchange of pleasantries or idle chit-chat? How many times did you allow others to interrupt you because your personality and conditioning dictated that another's needs came before yours? It is a trap we can fall into too easily. Just remember: This is your time and no one else should "spend" it.

Begin by planning your day with careful consideration to priorities — including your work schedule, time with your family, personal time, and leisure activities. In planning your work schedule, look at the tasks that produce worthwhile and high profits. Try to eliminate activities that contribute to low productivity and lead to frustration.

Four key ideas to keep in mind as you work and develop your Specialty Gift Basket Business are:

1. Planning provides direction for controlling the time to develop your business.

2. Knowledge of how effectively you use your time shows you how to develop the growth of your business.

3. Writing out your time plan and goals provides the motivation necessary to get you into action and makes the business fun to run.

4. Writing out your time plan will help you effectively produce expected results and provide you with a balance of time for work, health, recreation, and relationships.

## Plan Ahead To Save Time

In order to realize the highest profits and satisfy the most customers possible, you must plot out a course of action in advance with regard to:

* Purchasing Inventory

* Promotion and Advertising

* Creating

* Presentation (the sale)

* Delivery

For all major holidays, you should plan at least two months in advance. The Christmas season commands more lead time. You should usually have ideas and basket themes formulated by June for the Christmas holidays, so you can begin ordering in July.

Some general guidelines for preparation involve:

☐ Designing at least four basic types of baskets in three price ranges for both male and female customers

☐ Ordering merchandise early

☐ Setting sales goals

☐ Deciding how many baskets you can create and deliver in a day or a week, etc.

☐ Deciding if you need additional help and who will be doing deliveries

☐ Planning your promotional campaign — open house, brochures, newspapers, radio or direct mail

☐ Targeting corporate accounts early — October 1 for Christmas, January 1 for Valentine's Day, etc.

☐ Budgeting for inventory, advertising and mailings. Can you make up several baskets in advance and store them properly?

☐ Having all your proper basket embellishments on hand. Several weeks in advance, prepare your baskets.

    (a) Make all your handmade bows.

    (b) Gift wrap products for inclusion in baskets.

    (c) Line baskets and add filler.

    (d) Enhance basket handles with chosen decor.

Organize all your holiday merchandise in one place. Make trips to your wholesalers in June and purchase all the ornaments, berries, dried floral, etc. Find unique items to embellish your baskets for the holidays. Stock up on ribbon (from 1/4-inch to very wide), bows and enclosure cards. List all the extras that you will need for creating many baskets for the holidays. If you have the time, it is wise to look through a couple of craft magazines for creative hints and ideas for special holiday bows, unique ornaments and handcrafted items that will make your baskets stand far ahead of any competition. If you are fortunate enough to live in or near an area that has pine trees, gather as many pine cones as you can when they are in season. Make sure you get clean ones. If you want to go one step further, spray your cones with a high-gloss varnish (available in craft/supply stores).

Determine promotion and finalize dates. Make a decision as to how you are going to promote the gift baskets. Have your brochure ready for print and your customer and targeted market list available. Have a date and invitation ready for Holiday Open House. Have all necessary supplies and ingredients for baskets ready for assembly — such as plenty of wax for the hot glue gun, excelsior or filler, and plastic wrap for "packaging" the baskets. An example of a yearly planning guide is in Appendix A.

*"When one has much to put in them, a day has a hundred pockets."*
                        — Friedreich Nietzsche

**Chapter 6**

# Establishing your market and gift basket themes

**B**efore you plan your "Key Inventory Shopping List," you should have your start-up budget and know who your market is. Then you can sit down with a pencil and paper and start "brainstorming" ideas and themes for your baskets. This chapter will help spark your creative mind to come up with your own themes.

*"Creation comes before distribution — or there will be nothing to distribute!"*

— Ayn Rand

## Establishing Your Market

**I**f you can anticipate your market, ideas and inventory will be easier to plan. If you cannot define your market at the start, do some research or experimental marketing to define the type of customer who will buy your gift baskets. There is a mixture of people in all areas of the country. Some of you will target the more up-scale customers who are sophisticated with gourmet palates. Or you might find that the easiest client to reach may be less affluent, enjoy family environment and prefer the more homespun gift items.

If you find that your market is young urban professionals (age 25-44) with incomes over $20,000, your designs will be planned around their casual, yet sophisticated lifestyles — gift basket items that reflect good taste and are functional. Ask yourself the following questions:

☐ Do I need to do some background work in targeting my market and create a customer profile? This is entirely up to the individual. Maybe you are aware whom you will be targeting and already have an idea of how they buy; what their needs are, taste preference, and so forth. If you don't have a target market, here are some suggestions:

- Observe the buying habits of shoppers in your area.

- Estimate their general income bracket.

- Locate the areas they live in.

- Decide what area you want to target — residential neighborhoods, business or corporate.

- Estimate the average age of the people you will target. Is this a neighborhood of younger people who have small children, etc.?

## Think About Themes

**W**hat do you enjoy? Are your friends, acquaintances and neighbors inclined to have similar tastes? You need to look at their preferences. If they closely match yours, it is easier to create your basket themes. Trust yourself and your reactions. You don't need to be an artist to recognize beautiful art. You need to establish a habit of constantly seeking out good ideas and design. If something immediately creates a positive reaction in you, it usually will do the same for your customer.

☐ Ask yourself these questions:

- If I were recuperating from surgery in the hospital, what kind of a gift basket would I enjoy?

- What would my husband, son, daughter, mother or father enjoy?

- If I am a working mother, what would give me pleasure to receive for a 30th or 40th birthday present?

- If I were to receive a basket for Secretaries' Day, what would I enjoy receiving? Something edible? A "Kick Back and Relax" basket with a split of sparkling cider, goblet, truffles, candle and special bath products to take the stress out of my day?

- Ascertain what products are more or less generic and can cross over into many themes. These are the items that you will want to have on hand all the time.

☐ Write down all the special occasions you can think of and be prepared to have some of these in your gift basket line. The most common special occasions are: Birthday, Anniversary, Get-well, Thank You, New Baby, Wedding, Apology, I Love You, Congratulations, Retirement, New Home or Housewarming, and Sympathy, and all the ethnic ones you can think of.

☐ What seasonal items and colors do I need to coordinate the basket theme?

*"A man would do well to carry a pencil in his pocket and write down the thoughts of the moment. Those that come unsought are commonly the most valuable and should be secured, because they seldom return."*
— Francis Bacon

## Seasonal Themes

Gift basket themes fall into specific categories. The main categories are seasonal — Fall, Winter, Spring, and Summer. Always remember that seasonal themes can be blended in with the other theme types to enhance the decor of your baskets.

### Fall

Capture this beautiful time of the year in your basket design by using the vibrant colors of autumn — oranges, golds, browns, and reds. Use preserved autumn leaves, miniature pumpkins, gourds and dried corn available in floral and craft supply stores.

In September there is Labor Day, Grandparent's Day, Rosh Hashanah, and Yom Kippur. October brings Boss's Day, Columbus Day, and, of course, Halloween. In November you will be busy with Thanksgiving — a great time for people to give baskets.

# CALENDAR OF HOLIDAYS & SPECIAL EVENTS

**J**ANUARY
- [ ] New Year's Day
- [ ] Super Bowl

**F**EBRUARY
- [ ] Black History Month
- [ ] Lincoln's Birthday
- [ ] Valentine's Day
- [ ] Washington's Birthday

**M**ARCH
- [ ] St. Patrick's Day

**A**PRIL
- [ ] April Fools' Day
- [ ] Passover
- [ ] Easter (sometimes falls in March)
- [ ] Secretaries' Day and Week

**M**AY
- [ ] Mother's Day
- [ ] Memorial Day

**J**UNE
- [ ] Father's Day
- [ ] Graduations & Weddings

**J**ULY
- [ ] Independence Day

**S**EPTEMBER
- [ ] Labor Day
- [ ] Grandparent's Day
- [ ] Jewish New Year (or October)
- [ ] Yom Kippur (or October)

**O**CTOBER
- [ ] Boss's Day
- [ ] Halloween

**N**OVEMBER
- [ ] Thanksgiving Day

**D**ECEMBER
- [ ] Hanukkah
- [ ] Christmas
- [ ] New Year's Eve

## Winter

This time of year could be your busiest with Hanukkah, Christmas, and New Year. You will want to think about holiday colors for Christmas such as greens, reds, silver and golds and embellishing your baskets with artfully tied Christmas ribbon, ornaments (whether handcrafted, or manufactured), pine cones, berries, cinnamon sticks, bells, napkins and place mats in festive holiday colors. You can take advantage of the wonderful aromas of the season by featuring potpourri (cinnamon, bayberry, woodsy, pine, etc.). We suggest green and red baskets, with the handles wrapped in eucalyptus which emits a lovely fragrance, and enhances the total look of the basket. You can also decorate with fresh boughs of Douglas fir, pine, cedar, a fragrant touch to add the right seasonal flair. You will be surprised how many baskets you sell!

If you are doing Hanukkah baskets, remember that blue and white are the predominant colors. Also, there are certain food items that are not acceptable. Check at the local synagogue to see if they recommend an outlet that carries items appropriate for this holiday and that can be included in your basket.

New Year's baskets can be imaginative and fun. Bring out the glitz and glitter, horns, confetti and champagne — let your baskets ring in the New Year with a lasting impression.

After the holidays, during January, February and March, themes take on the appropriate colors for Valentine's Day, Washington's Birthday and St. Patrick's Day in March.

To accentuate the romance of Valentine's Day, you can think about hearts, lace, cupids and flowers using the traditional colors red, pink and white. Picnic baskets with a romantic theme would be appropriate. Single-stem roses, whether silk, chocolate, or real in a crystal bud vase are always popular. Candles, a bottle of sparkling wine, cheese and crackers denote a romantic evening at home. You can purchase Valentine's cakes, cookies, special desserts, or other chocolates and candies to laden your baskets with the message of love.

Be creative with every occasion. Special orders might call for research into an historical period like Washington's birthday. Take a trip to the library to get ideas.

St. Patrick's Day gives you the opportunity to be creative with shades of green and white along with a mix of traditional Irish items. You can purchase festive decor for this holiday at any supply wholesaler or craft store. Another idea is to use an Irish linen look or Four-Leaf Clover plants, either real or made of silk.

## Spring

Spring is a season to welcome change, renewal, and fresh growing things. This season includes Easter, Secretaries' Day, Secretaries' Week (an opportunity to remind your corporate accounts about giving baskets to their secretaries), Mother's Day, Cinco de Mayo, and Memorial Day at the end of May. This is the time of year to add spring colors to your baskets with silk or fresh flowers like daffodils, daisies, Easter lilies and roses, to name a few. Dried flowers in a delicate lace cone can add a burst of spring.

Easter baskets can be a joy to create. Decorate hollow eggs with rickrack, sequins and other decor. Stuffed animals such as Easter bunnies, add a playful and whimsical touch to the baskets. Lavenders, pinks, greens, and yellows and other pastels are appropriate colors for this time of the year. Don't be afraid to work with the more dramatic colors in deeper hues such as bright blue, apricot/peach, forest green, grape — tapestry colors — they add boldness and excitement with a different slant on the season!

If you are going to create Easter baskets for children, it is advisable to keep them in the $10-$20 price range. You can use stuffed bunnies, Easter candy, pens, pencils, crayons, chalk, books, color books and inexpensive games or puzzles. Specialty Easter baskets can include Peter Rabbit and Beatrix Potter items. Little girls appreciate hair bows and barrettes, and little boys go for cars, and baseball cards.

The end of spring brings Mother's Day and you can incorporate the lovely spring colors with the other themes such as Victorian, Southwest, gardening, cooking, sewing — items that are beautiful, feminine and useful. This is also a good time to have a "Spring Fling" — an Open House to introduce your new line for the coming summer and fall months and to have a sale on merchandise that you need to clear out.

## Summer

June starts the summer season with Father's Day. A time to choose the more masculine colors — blue, grey, brown, black, and purple — colors that go very handsomely with subtle designs depicting a sport or hobby theme.

The Fourth of July can be quite festive using red, white, and blue with stars and stripes and lots of hoopla! This is a perfect time to tie into a barbecue basket, fishing, picnic theme, or maybe something nautical. Find out what father likes best.

Specialty gift baskets are certainly not limited to a particular season. They are easily tailored to suit the theme of any gift-giving occasion.

## Ideas For Special Occasions

Special occasion themes encompass: birthday, new baby, get-well, thank you, anniversary, wedding, new home, congratulations, retirement, bon voyage and many more.

You can divide these themes into categories such as male, female, child, romantic, humorous, and friendship. Break these categories into price ranges — low, medium and high.

For Mother's Day create a British Tea Garden Basket with cups and saucer, yummy morsels imported from Britain, such as English tea biscuits, jams, preserves, scones, and teas. Twist ivy around the handle to exude the feeling of having tea in an English garden.

For Father's Day, assemble a barbecue basket using all the utensils, mitt, apron, gourmet barbecue sauce, cookbook, matches, wire brush, and any other appropriate items.

Wedding baskets are popular gifts. For example, create a theme by choosing a white heart-shaped basket. Include a picture frame either in white or brass, white padded coat hangers, white sachet bags or potpourri for the home with a lovely container; soaps, drawer liners — use items that both the bride and groom can use. Decorate with a spray of white berries, white ribbon on the handle, two doves, one on each side of the handle with a thin, 1/4-inch ribbon connected to their beaks. Add contrast with another color such as deep rose or blue (add silk flowers). The important point to remember is that you want it to be visually bridal!

## Product Themes

Product themes include specialty food or gourmet baskets — such as the Chocolate Lover Basket, Perfect Pasta Basket, No Cholesterol Basket, Fresh Herb Basket, English Tea Basket, and a Breakfast Basket. These product themes can be combined with regional themes like South-of-the-Border Basket, New Orleans/Creole Basket, or Italian/Pasta Basket.

Create gift baskets using a state or regional theme. This is a perfect gift for out-of-state visitors. Find unique products indigenous to your area and create a theme around them. For example, almonds and rice (and wild rice) are products of the Sacramento Valley, and Sacramento is close to Napa Valley which offers a wide range of wines, wine jams, jellies, and other related products. If you live in a coastal area, focus in on a nautical theme using smoked salmon, or anything "fishing related" — toy sailboats, sea gulls, netting, shells, etc. — a Seafarer Basket would be a catchy basket for this area.

*"The pioneer with the new idea*
*Must start it operating.*
*With this feat he will beat*
*Those still contemplating"*
  *— Anonymous*

Is there a specialized craft indigenous to your area? An issue of *Glad Tidings* suggested a basket using the Mason-Dixon Theme based on historical fact that over 60% of the Civil War was fought in Virginia. To capture this "time" in history, one can use blues and greys for the colors and food products from the South such as smoked ham, ciders, and spoon bread; and from the North, maple products, pancake mix, and conserves. Add mini Confederate and Yankee Flags for the finishing touch.

There are many unique specialty food products in the marketplace such as wonderful dressings, coffees, and teas. There are "to-die-for" desserts such as Oreo cookie crumb cake and a wide selection of decadent chocolates, syrups and sauces. The dessert sauces to choose from are unbelievable. These sauces are definitely a hit for the gourmet palate, like Black Forest Melba Sauce. There is a vast selection of nuts for the nut lover such as delicious cashew-Brazil nut buttercrunch.

Consumers are increasingly aware of the importance of nutrition for good health. There are products available that are organically grown, chemical free, and have no preservatives or additives. These include cholesterol-free chocolate gourmet brownies with no animal fats or hydrogenated shortening (all natural). You can purchase healthy and tasty sauces that are table-ready such as tomato conserve, and a cashew ginger sauce.

There are delectable soup mixes that will enhance the taste buds of your customers. They are ready to fix and eat, which makes this product even more attractive.

Bread and breakfast mixes like scones are a terrific way to tie into a "Breakfast Basket" theme. The list goes on and on. It is definitely a good idea to frequent the Gourmet Shows in the city closest to you to continually find new and unique foods with eye-appealing packaging and to keep yourself state-of-the-art with your gourmet gift concepts and themes.

For example, with the lure of the Southwestern influence, there is an indigenous regional cuisine that has evolved over centuries. Southwestern foods called Tex Mex or Mexican, express a vast array of exciting colors with greens and reds of chilies, the golden yellows of corn, and the warm hues of beans and rice.

A good mix of ingredients for a Southwestern basket would include: tortilla chips, various salsas and sauces, chili, nacho cheese sauce, beans, and chili peppers. You can enhance this festive basket by bringing in pottery-type taco holders, etc. Many seasonings pertinent to this ethnic cuisine can be added.

In addition, there are many new sauces and condiments for stir frying in the specialty food market for the Eastern or Oriental theme.

A few pointers to remember when working with food items:

Try to complement food and beverage baskets with the appropriate accoutrements, such as, coffee cups with special flavored coffees; glasses with beverages; cutting board and knife for cheese; tablecloth for picnic, etc.

Don't blend certain scents such as potpourri sachets with food items unless stored in an airtight container. Also, don't use perfumed bath soaps in food baskets; they just don't mix!

## Idea Themes

Idea or Concept Themes evolve around topics including Sports, Time/Era, Area or Feeling. They can be centered around Victorian, Southwest, Country French, Americana, Western, Contemporary, Traditional or Renaissance themes or even horoscopes. This gets into the  more personalized or custom-designed area of the business. When you are giving your sales presentation, whether over the phone or in person, have a question checklist with which to go over the needs of the buyer and the recipient. Ask what the recipient's favorite colors are? Is he or she involved in sports? What profession? How is their home decorated? What era? Do they have pets (animal or bird theme)? From these questions, you can extract a certain element of their personality to help you personalize the basket decoration.

## *BIRTHDAY IDEAS*

**Male Adult**:

Sports or hobby related
Professional (executive, traveler, attorney, sales)
(*Example: For the "Traveling Man" —a collection
 of men's grooming aids and scents in a travel pouch*).
Humorous
General (practical) - any man will relate to

**Teenagers**:

Latest fad
Sports or hobby related
Male or female

**Female Adult:**

Sentimental/Thoughtful
Sports or hobby related
Humorous
General (practical) any woman
would enjoy

**New Baby**

Mom, Dad and Baby makes "three"
Shower - Mom and Baby
New Father
Just for Baby

As you list and categorize each special occasion, you will note that you can cross-reference many themes and ideas.

In profiling your birthday baskets for the male, think about males you know — your husband, friends, and relatives. What type of work are they in? What sports do they enjoy? Most men like televised sports such as football, basketball, baseball and golf. Most of them work and appreciate achieving status in business and in the community; they like physical activities such as jogging, tennis, golf, walking and working out. What do they like to eat and drink? In selecting items for the man, remember that they appreciate gifts that can be consumed. A large majority of the male population travels. They tend to buy gifts that are edible, drinkable, usable — and, the sooner, the better.

Women tend to be collectors of items of sentimental value; keepsakes and items decorative and ornamental in design.

As you go through each special occasion, you will come up with a grandiose list of categories and theme ideas from which you can create your key inventory shopping list.

## EXAMPLES OF BASKET THEMES

**Breakfast Basket:**
Crepe, pancake, waffle or scone mix
Syrup
Jams
Napkins
Coffee cup
Teas/Deep roasted blend or flavored coffee

**Pasta Basket:**
Red and white checked napkins
Shelf-stable pasta
Seasonings or mixes
Garlic press
Spaghetti fork
Olive oil
Salad dressing or vinegar
Sun dried tomatoes
Biscotti
Wooden spoon
Wine glasses
Favorite beverage
Wine opener
Wine collar
Breadsticks

**South-of-the Border Basket:**
Chili or chili mix
Chips and salsa
Bean dip
Wine glasses & favorite beverage
Napkins to match color theme
Mexican pottery for salsa (optional)
Strand of chili peppers to decorate
Tex Mex seasonings

**Birthday Basket for Lady:**
Sparkling cider
Napkin
Potpourri
Shell night light
Stationery, cookbook, note cards or recipes
Flavored coffee

**New Orleans/Creole Basket:**
*(Combination Spanish, French, Creole & Cajun)*
Creole mustards
Barbeque Sauce
Cajun products or peppery sauces/seasonings
Mixes of rice and beans
Napkins to match
Wine glasses
Favorite beverage
Small cast-iron skillet (optional)

**Decadent Delight Basket:**
Napkins
Ice cream dishes
Ice cream scoop
Dessert Sauces and Toppings
Wafers or "Pirolette"
Napkins

**Gardening Basket:**
Gloves
Mini indoor gardening tools
Watering can
Seeds or herbs
Potted plant
Plant book
Plant food

**Bath Basket:**
Potpourri (sachets or other)
Washclothes
Gels, bubble bath or decorative soaps
Candle and holder
Good tape, book or book of poems
Body lotion
Sponges

**Picnic Basket:**
Napkins
Tablecloth or placemats
Nice plastic plates, or paper with wicker holders
Utensils
Cutting board and knife
Wine glasses

Chocolates
Silk flowers and baby's breath to embellish

**Sports/Tennis Theme Basket:**
Tennis balls
Visor
Plastic water jug
Mist bottle
Wrist bands
Tennis magazine for current month

**Corporate Basket:**
Napkin
Flavored coffee
Coffee cups or mug
Brass letter opener, shoehorn or other "executive toy"
Travel accessories
Note cards, reminders, etc.

## SUGGESTED INVENTORY LIST

**Baskets**
All sizes and shapes, different weaves, textures materials, and colors.

**Glassware and China:**
Wine glasses and champagne glasses
Coffee cups or mugs
Candleholders
Salt & pepper shakers (optional). *You can pick up unique sets at thrift stores. Try discount stores — look for sales or order from a catalog where you can purchase other inventory.*

**Serving Pieces, Utensils & Kitchen Gadgets:**
Cheese or cutting board
Wooden spoons
Garlic press
Pasta scoop
Wine bottle opener or corkscrew
Eating utensils (if you are doing Picnic Baskets)
Ice Cream Scoop (if doing Ice Cream Baskets)

**Bath Items:**
Washcloths
 Potpourri (sachets or bags). *You can buy in quantity and then transfer to small ornamental containers, or easily make your own sachets.*
Bath salts (optional)
Sprays (optional)
Bubble bath (optional)
Bath gels and perfumed bath foams (optional)
Bar soap *(decorate with lace ribbon and wrap like a gift package. You can also purchase small dish soaps in different shapes such as sea shells, animals, flowers, etc.)*
Soap leaves (optional). *You can buy small packages for traveling from a sales rep or order through catalog.*
Bath lotions (optional)
Other bath accessories that are appropriate

**Linens:**
Cloth napkins in assorted colors
Place mats & tablecloths (optional)
Plastic tablecloth (checked-print great in Picnic baskets.)
Hand and dish towels - bath and kitchen theme baskets.
Potholders (optional) - unique potholders can embellish a gift basket quite nicely!

**Paper Items:** If ordered in quantity, these items are nice additions
Stationery
Note cards
Journals
Address books
Recipe cards
Cookbooks (paperback) If ordered in quantity, these items are always a nice addition to the baskets.

**Child:**

Pail, truck, toolbox or handmade wooden critter make cute containers
Coloring books/activity books
Crayons/washable finger paints
Puzzle
Children's book
Tapes

**Baby Items:**

Shampoo, soaps, powder, etc.
Teething rings and rattles
Baby blocks *(Can be purchased at large craft supply or discount store.)*
Receiving blankets (optional) You can use them to line higher-priced baby baskets.
Stuffed animals *(A must in a baby basket. You can buy wholesale or retail when marked down. Other specialty baby items can be ordered through various catalogs.)*

**Other:**

Padded hangers
Picture frames
Wine collars and coasters
Candles
Live plants (purchase as needed)

**High-End Items:**

Brass items such as letter openers (optional)
Small silver serving pieces such as candy dish
China or crystal serving pieces
Shoehorn
Crystal bud vase
Crystal candleholder
Leather items: photo carriers, key chain cases, coin purse manicure set, etc.

**Novelty and Unique Items:**

Shell nightlights (optional)
Holiday ornaments
Handcrafted items *(from someone you know or artisans in your area that sell at craft fairs.)*
Novelty items *(for sports theme, special*

*holiday and occasions such as Easter, weddings, anniversary)*

**Other Optional Items:**

Plant seeds
Gardening tools
Gardening gloves
Kitchen gadgets
Sports items: wrist bands for tennis, tennis balls, golf balls, sport visors

**Food Items:**

Almonds or nuts
Cookies and small dessert cakes with a 6-month shelf life
Chocolates, truffles, etc.
Flavored coffees and teas
Package mixes: crepes, waffles, pancakes, scones, soup, lentils and beans.
Crackers
Preserves: jams, jellies, honey, marmalade.
Condiments: Mustards, oils, dressings, vinegar, spices and seasonings
Smoked salmon or oysters
Meat sauces and marinades
Specialty food items indigenous to area or culture, i.e., Southwest or Tex-Mex, Italian
Unique food items (such as corn popped on the cob, scones, quail eggs, truffles, old-fashioned Swiss licorice).

Some of these items can be purchased from volume discount stores at reasonable prices for minimum quantity orders. However, you will most likely get better volume discounts buying through manufacturer's catalogs, or from their representatives and distributors. Additionally, you can purchase most items at gift shows, and gourmet and fancy food shows.

**Chapter 7**

# *INITIAL INVENTORY BUYING AND STORAGE*

## Compiling a Key Inventory Shopping List

In the last chapter we showed you how to compile an inventory list by deciding on themes and targeting your market. In this chapter we will cover buying procedures and options and suggest the best ways for storing your products.

Once you have established your Key Inventory Shopping List, you are ready to order products from a manufacturer or wholesaler. Buying at wholesale generally requires the buyer to purchase goods and products in volume and at a price discount of 30% to 60% below normal or suggested retail. Purchasing products from retail outlets, discount stores, crafts persons, swap meets, and thrift stores allows you to buy in smaller quantities. You will probably do both, and in this chapter we will give you pointers on buying your baskets and supplies.

## Ordering

The first mistake that new business owners tend to make when ordering inventory is that they overbuy. Since overstocking can help kill a business, we will discuss causes of surplus inventory and how to avoid it. Some small businesses will be urged by the manufacturer to take a large quantity at an extra discount — say 10%. However, if it takes you over a year to move this larger quantity, it is not worth buying in volume for the discount unless you know that you have an account that is placing a large order, therefore using the greater part of the inventory.

Inventory management is an important factor in the gift basket business and we will pass on some of our "secrets" to you. Once you get the feel of how your clientele orders, purchasing inventory will become easy. The first time around is always the most difficult.

Attend gift shows, gourmet shows, and gift basket trade shows in your area and subscribe to *Gifts & Decorative Accessories Magazine* or any of the gift industry publications that keep you apprised of what trends are happening in the gift industry and make you "state-of-the-art" in your buying and creating.

## What to Look for When You Buy

Look for the companies that carry a quality basket line. Find a company with a large selection of baskets made from different materials, various weaves and colors and a wide variety of styles. Search for companies that offer not only baskets, but other items that can be used to decorate your gift baskets. The more items you can order from one company the better, because you are paying a one-time freight charge and saving time. More and more wholesalers are catering to the gift basket business by offering a variety of items and packaging that meets the needs of the gift basket retailer.

When purchasing baskets, a minimum order for buying wholesale (at cost) with most gift basket companies is usually $100 to $250 on the first order, and $100 minimum on reorders. A handling charge between $5 to $10 is customary for all orders under $50. As a new account, you will probably be paying C.O.D. with a deposit. This is changing with the popularity and number of gift basket businesses blooming around the country. Manufacturers are beginning to cater to this sector.

Once you establish credit with various companies, the payment terms are usually "2%/10 days, Net 30" from invoice date. The "2%/10 days" means that you can deduct 2% if you pay on the 10th instead of the 30th day. A service charge of 1.5% per month is the norm on assessing past due balances. You should always take cash discounts when paying bills.

To establish credit with a basket company, you usually need to furnish at least three trade references with complete addresses and account numbers. As a first-time purchaser of baskets, you pay cash on the first order. Advise them you are getting established and would like to build your credit references.

Order items that can be used year-round and have a few seasonal items that can be used year after year, i.e., Valentine's Day supplies.

One of the keys to being successful in this business is to tailor your inventory qualitatively and quantitatively to the particular demands of your potential market. A familiar marketing phrase that has been used by various industry leaders and that sticks in our mind at all times is "we aim to please."

It is important to build your inventory in a reasonably healthy balance with sales and to maintain that balance within the ever-changing demand and supply conditions. You need to concentrate on providing your customers with a range of choices within theme categories of merchandise without overstocking a slow seller and understocking fast-moving items. If you are continually moving inventory, you are making profits!

## Basket Buying Options

When you start to purchase your baskets, you will find that you have many choices depending on your budget and clientele. There are import companies such as Palacek (San Francisco) that are considered the "Mercedes-Benz" of the basket industry. They are top-of-the-line in baskets and that is their niche in the marketplace. They strive to obtain uniqueness and exclusivity in their product by doing some of their own finishing and reprocessing and thereby always offering quality items.

Importers frequently offer new designs in baskets. They carry new colors, textures and weave to reflect freshness in lines. Some companies handle exclusive lines such as Country French and "designer baskets." There are a vast array of finishes such as bamboo and bark. The more avant-garde finishes are white-wash, metallic, a painted-motif and fabric accents adding drama and bold excitement to basket design.

The basic style basket is still popular for utilitarian purposes such as a container for towels, magazines, recipes and other household items. Because baskets have become very much a part of interior decor, they are taking on dramatic new shapes as demand becomes more sophisticated. Order your baskets so about 10% are high-line items. The important point to remember is that a basket's function has become more important to the consumer than its ethnic background. Obtain catalogs from several basket manufacturers so you can compare quality, price, and diversification of product line.

## Other Buying Options

There are terrific bargains at discount stores, grocery stores, and outlets. For example, if you are going to buy inventory in the area of kitchen-related items, you can purchase an array of gadgets at a discount store such as "Pic and Save" (i.e., slotted spoons, openers, apple slicer, spatula, egg slicer, vegetable steamer, utensils for picnic baskets, nutcrackers, melon scoops, ice cream scoops, measuring cups, and measuring spoons). Track down the best buys in your area — even garage sales can behold some hidden treasures.

Another possibility for finding merchandise is to frequent the craft fairs and find unique, quality items that are handcrafted and handmade by artists in your area.

There are many "Ma and Pa" businesses that offer unique products.

> *Prior to the holidays one year, a car dealer in the area wanted to purchase unique gifts for his clients. We located and purchased wooden reindeer that were handmade by an elderly man whose wife hand-painted and signed each reindeer. This immediately became a collectable and intriguing item for the car dealer and his clients. For the "Bloomin' Baskets" touch, we filled each reindeer with two kinds of flavored coffees with our own label, arranged through a local coffee wholesaler/retailer. The coffee emitted a very nice and appealing aroma. We included a dessert, a Christmas ornament, and embellished the reindeer with a spray of eucalyptus, berries, cinnamon, and other Christmas greenery. They were a hit!*

Thrift stores are a terrific source for finding unique items for gift baskets inexpensively. Be sure to stop by your local .99 store, if available in your area, and pick up great bargains on small items and unique gadgets. Quality merchandise can be found once you develop an eye for sorting through the "junk" and finding the "gems." Go to several thrift stores in your area and choose one or two that have consistently decent merchandise. Once you sift through the undesirable merchandise, you will be able to spot the appropriate items for the baskets. For example, salt and pepper shakers, glassware and sets of glassware; jewelry and beads for decor; scarves to tie around the handle to create special effects; toys and many other items can enhance the themes of your basket. Remember, one person's idea of junk is another person's treasure.

## Purchasing Food Items

If you are a newcomer to specialty foods, you should stock items that have a good shelf life such as preserves, condiments, cookies, and candies. For the fall/winter holidays, specialty foods should be ordered before the end of September to be well stocked. Order from suppliers that can give a quick "turn-around time" if you need to order more for a special corporate account. Always be mindful of perishable vs. non-perishable items, location, shipping factor, and minimum orders.

## Perishables

By its very definition, perishables can make the cautious even more cautious. Perishables are: "food stuffs that are easily injured or liable to decay or spoil." Be very careful when ordering food items for your baskets. In the gift basket industry, perishables can be considered any food prepared or packaged without preservatives, or any food that spoils easily. Among the favorites are: fruit, breads, cookies, cakes, confections, chocolates, fragile cheeses and some canned or packaged meats. Check local and state laws regarding any food products. Certain requirements may be enforceable such as refrigeration, inspections, special sinks, or shelving.

The secret to success with perishables is freshness so order less, and order more frequently. When ordering food products, always check the package or shelf date or check the items out with the salesperson representing a particular line. Ask the supplier how long a certain item has been in their warehouse. Select a supplier who continually receives, and sends their customers fresh shipments of perishable products.

If you are using homemade items, they can sell for triple their cost of making. Check and see what foods need to be refrigerated within a certain time frame. For instance, certain boneless hams need to be refrigerated immediately upon receipt as the shelf life without refrigeration is 10 days and under refrigeration, 8 weeks.

Some states do not allow the handling of fruits, vegetables or unpacked foods. If this is the case, you can still present beautiful and appealing specialty food baskets and not deal in hard line perishables. Use shelf-stable cheeses and sausages, especially around the holidays. Whether you stick to non-perishables, semi-perishables, or highly perishable products will most likely depend entirely on your customer demands. (See source list in Appendix B.)

## *Ordering for the Executive Gift Basket*

When stocking gifts for the corporate gift basket, remember to scale your products up or down depending on the set price limit. A business may want 40 gift baskets at $35.00 each for its salespeople, while another company may order 50 baskets at $75.00 each to give to top management and executives of other companies.

According to *Gift Basket Review*, the following are popular choices for corporate gift baskets:

- Specialty coffees and tea

- Non-perishable gourmet specialty foods such as caviar, smoked salmon, smoked oysters, smoked hams, imported cheeses, preserves, condiments, nuts, chocolates, truffles, confection, regional or ethnic food groupings accompanied with appropriate accessories, recipe and cookbooks

- Collectibles such as china or porcelain, sterling silver or gold utensils, personalized items and monogrammed stemware

- High-end desk accessories such as paperweights, pen and pencil sets, desk-size appointment books, calendars, business card holders, etc.

- Coordinated personal items such as key holders, money clips, grooming accessories, tie clips, blank journals, note cards, stationery, etc. toiletries and fragrances, adult games and puzzles or electronic "toys"

# Storage of Inventory

The way you store your inventory is very important. Storage must be neatly organized to facilitate your entire process of assembling baskets. We will cover some ideas that worked well for *Those Bloomin' Baskets, etc.* and you can adapt them to create storage room for your own needs according to the house, condo or apartment from which you will be working.

## *Storing the Baskets*

The best method of storing baskets is to hang them. Use a garage, basement, extra room, or a well-protected shed to hang your baskets. Hanging baskets from the ceiling enables you to spot the basket that you need quickly, to take inventory more easily, and still not impose upon your living quarters and valuable square footage in your home.

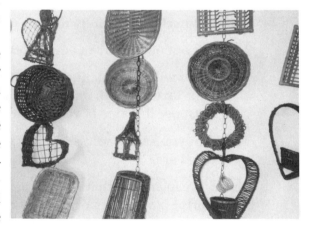

Purchase plant hooks for the larger baskets and cup hooks for the smaller baskets. Affix them in neat rows to the rafters in the garage. (Don't try to do this in one "fell swoop" as you can become dizzy and wear out your arm — get some help!) This is just a one-time laborious duty so proceed with the thought that it will all be worth it.

You can also run rope or link chains from one beam to another and tie the baskets to the rope or links with a baggie tie. If you do not have a garage or ceiling in an extra room, affix plant hooks on an empty wall and run chain links (as used for swag lamps) down the wall as pictured above (you can probably get five to eight chains along one wall). Hang the baskets on the links with baggie ties, with pipe cleaner cut into pieces, or if you want to get fancy, use ribbon. Whether you hang your baskets from the ceiling or down a wall, you will find that it adds texture and personality to the area — definitely a decorative technique and a great way to store your baskets.

If you do not hang your baskets and use a storage shed or the garage, make sure that you place plastic covering or a tarp on the floor to protect the baskets from getting damp.

You might have an extra room that you can make visually attractive and also use as a storage place for the baskets. For example, decorate the walls in a room using tiny nails to hang unique-shaped baskets and smaller items. You will receive many compliments on this wall-basket decor and it does add interest and texture to the room — but most important, what a wonderful way to store the baskets!

You can also stack the baskets in various areas, but it is very difficult to spot one if you need it quickly. Find an area in your condo, house or apartment where you can utilize the space in the most efficient manner. Be creative. We are sure you can think of many more ways to store your baskets.

To determine where to store your other inventory items, the first step is to consider the following:

☐ Is it in close proximity to your work area?

☐ Is it out of the way of your everyday living needs?

☐ If you will be deducting this particular area for business usage on your taxes, certain specifications must be met. Remember, you must use this area of your home exclusively for business.

☐ Can you easily access items from your inventory in this designated area?

☐ Store in an area that will not harm or damage your inventory. If storing jams, jellies, or other food items, temperature is an important factor and dampness can effect many items so think this out carefully.

A great solution for storing the diversified merchandise for your gift baskets is to invest in bins. Shop wisely by scanning all the special advertising inserts in your local newspaper from various volume discount stores, and find who is running a special on storage bins. Invest in the large bins on casters that stack so that you can move them around with ease, or use the regular plastic, stackable bins. You can purchase these bins for a very reasonable price and it is an excellent way to keep your inventory neat and organized. You can also purchase the large, plastic, square crates (2 for $5 on special) for storing cookbooks, and other items. Use one bin for 1-3 items depending upon quantity and size.

For example, in one stackable bin, put items for a baby basket (shampoo, lotions, rattles, square wooden blocks with colored letters, small stuffed animals, baby books and receiving blankets). In another bin, store kitchen gadgets such as melon ballers, paring knives and measuring spoons for the kitchen baskets. Keep your bins organized according to your basket themes if possible.

You can store cloth napkins, place mats, linens and washcloths on hangers to save space. Store your food items on a shelf if you can. If you do not have a shelf in your closet or designated area, you might think of installing a 2 x 4 that lays on top of a hanger rod, or hang a shelf from a chain affixed to the ceiling to accommodate your specialty food items.

This will be a large part of your inventory so it is important that you use an area that is easy to access and that has an even temperature (to prevent spoilage, etc). If you must use your linen closet, you can install an extra piece of plywood on the floor to add more storage space. When you receive food items, such as jams, and jellies, stock them just as they do in a grocery store. Stack them so that all items are visible. Use every square inch of space.

## Storage of Supplies

### Filler (Excelsior)

Wherever you store your baskets, preferably in proximity to your work area, keep supplies such as excelsior (filler) near the baskets.

Excelsior can be messy so hold the basket that you are going to fill over the box or area that the excelsior is in.

> *Because we stored our baskets in the garage during one phase of the business, the plastic liner and filler were kept in the garage also. That way, we would line and fill all of the baskets for the first phase, and move them into the work area for the second phase of assembly to prevent tracking any filler into the living quarters.*

If your work space and storage of supplies are in the same area — you can be twice as efficient.

## Plastic Liner

Plastic liner can be bought in rolls of clear or colored plastic from a floral or craft supplier.

## Dried Florals

You will be using dried florals, such as baby's breath, to embellish your gift baskets. German statice, yarrow, eucalyptus, caspia, pods, pine cones, and other dried florals do take up space, so hang some of the dried flowers from the rafters.

Another good idea is to take a thin piece of plywood and have that handy person with a power drill make small holes so that the stems of one bouquet can fit. This is a very smart way to store dried florals as they are easily accessible and you always know exactly how much you have.

## Ribbon

The basket business requires lots of ribbon. You can build up your supply gradually. Buy ribbon in bolts (wholesale) from a craft store or from a wholesale florist. Notice how they display the ribbon they sell in their store. One of the easiest ways to store ribbon is to get about three or four wooden dowels or rods (like thin curtain rods), and either drill holes between two areas to support these dowels, or use a cup hook. Hang the chain links from the hook, and slip the rods inside. Another idea is to use sturdy plant hooks on two wooden dividers and slip a dowel or rod inside these hooks.

It is very important to organize your ribbon by color. This saves time when you assemble the baskets. Almost every basket you assemble will have a bow or ribbon and it is so nice just to pick your color and pull — no mess, no fuss, and no hunting around for that special ribbon you need.

## Silks

You will also be using silk florals to embellish your baskets. You can keep all your silks in one container and use this as a beautiful floral display in your home. You can buy some good quality silk flowers for decent prices that while being stored will add color and beauty to your home as well. You don't even have to be creative — just bunch all your silks together, place them in a tall container, and gently spread them out. (Please see source at end of book.)

*We have all our silks flowers sitting in an antique milk can. It is one of the major focal points in our living room.*

## Other Tools and Supplies That You Will Need

A hot glue gun is a must in the gift basket business. You can purchase this item at any craft supply, or wholesale florist store. You need to have plenty of hot wax on hand as this is what you will use to affix ribbons and other decor to the baskets.

Another piece of equipment that you might want to invest in is a shrink-wrap machine. You can probably get along without this item, but if you end up with large corporate orders it would come in handy. Supply items such as hot wax sticks, pipe cleaners, lace, netting material, floral picks, regular glue, wire cutters, wire, felt, scissors, string, tissue paper, fabric scraps, and enclosure cards should be stored close to your work area.

Another great idea for storing supplies is a hanging shoe bag. It hangs nicely in one end of the closet, keeping other areas available for the plastic storage bins. By using the shoe bag, all of your items are visible, organized, and easy to find.

# Inventory Control

**B**asic merchandising techniques are the foundation upon which profits depend. A widely accepted definition of merchandising is "the planning involved in marketing the right merchandise, at the right place and time, in the right quantities."

Any business that sells or manufactures goods and any service business that stocks parts must have some sort of inventory control. You must know what has been ordered, what is on hand, and when it is time to reorder. If you have a computer, keep your inventory "in memory."

Any time you purchase inventory, you must keep written records. We suggest that you follow one of these two procedures:

**(1)** When you place an order, record the quantity and the date of the order in the "ordered" column of a ledger sheet. When you receive the order, line out the entry in the Ordered column and enter the information in the "Received" column. Post the date you receive items. That way you will know how long it takes your suppliers to send you an item. If you receive only part of your order, record the undelivered back-ordered quantity and the original order date in the "Ordered" column.

**(2)** Keep the aforementioned items on an index card — one for each category. Keep the cards in an index box in the same manner you would file recipes. When you sell an item, keep track of what items went into the basket. This will become second nature when you see how easy it is to refer to the card when invoicing your customer. Everything that went into the basket is already recorded to arrive at a detailed pricing to the customer.

# Ordering Terminology

**T**here are a few key terms that are important to know in this industry, especially when ordering merchandise.

**Beginning Inventory** — goods on hand and available for sale to customers at the beginning of the accounting period.

**Cash Discount** — a reduction in price (usually 2% or less) offered by manufacturers and wholesalers to encourage customers to pay for merchandise within a specified discount period. This should be mentioned to you beforehand, but it usually appears on the invoice.

**Cost of Goods Sold** — a computation appearing as a separate section of an income statement showing the cost of goods sold during the period. This figure is computed by adding net delivered cost of merchandise purchases to beginning inventory to obtain cost of goods available for sale, and then deducting from this total the amount of the ending inventory . (This figure is usually equal to between 60 to 80 percent of net sales.)

**Ending Inventory** — goods still on hand and available for sale to customers at the end of the accounting period.

**F.O.B. Destination** — the seller bears the cost of shipping goods to the buyer's location. This is usually found on the purchase order or invoice that accompanies the order.

**F.O.B. Shipping Point** — the buyer of goods bears the cost of transportation from the seller's location to the buyer's location.

**Gross Profit on Sales** — revenue from sales minus cost of goods sold. In other words, gross profit is a percentage of sales. For example, if you want a 50 percent gross profit, you will have to mark up the purchase cost 100 percent. To get a gross profit of 40 percent, you will have to mark up the purchase cost about 65 percent. This mark-up percentage varies a great deal. Gross profit can be increased in a number of ways: (1) promoting a larger number of higher marked-up goods, (2) buying for less; (3) selling for more, and (4) stopping snafu leading to inventory shortages (you must control paperwork of shipping and billing documents).

**Keystone** — is an old term used in retailing and simply means that one buys at wholesale or a given price and then doubles their cost to establish the retail price to the customer.

**Net 30 days** — this is found on the invoice under the word "Terms" and means that if you pay your bill in full within the 30-day period of dated invoice, there will be no finance charge assessed. Any payment after this 30 day period (past due) will have a finance charge added.

**Operating Expenses** — includes both selling expenses and general administrative expenses deducted from gross profit on sales to determine net income.

**Physical Inventory** — the process of counting and pricing the merchandise on hand at a given date, usually the end of the accounting period.

**Selling Expenses** — expenses of marketing the product such as advertising, sales, salaries and delivery of merchandise to customers. This is a subdivision of operating expenses.

**Merchandise** — goods acquired by a business for resale to customers.

**Specific Identification Method** — this method assigns the actual purchase costs to the specific items purchased. You take the figures listed on the actual purchase invoices.

**Average-cost Method** — this method is computed by dividing the total cost of goods available for sale by the number of units available for sale.

**First-in, First-out Method** — this method is often referred to as "fifo" and based on the assumption that the first merchandise acquired is the first merchandise sold. Therefore, when using this method, your ending inventory consists of the most recently acquired goods.

**Last-in, First-out Method** — this method is often referred to as "lifo" and the premise behind this method is that the most recently acquired goods are sold first, and that the ending inventory consists of "old" goods acquired in the earliest purchases. Therefore the costs assigned to the cost of goods sold are relatively current because they stem from the most recent purchases.

The decision on which inventory evaluation method to use is a difficult one because the figure that is used is one that will be shown on the balance sheet and the income statement, which are two separate but very important documents. You may not have a reason in your gift basket business to ever have to produce either of these documents. But for basic comprehension, these two financial statements are intended for different purposes. The function of the inventory figure in the income statement is to permit a matching of costs and revenue. In the balance sheet the inventory and the other current assets are regarded as a measure of your company's ability to meet its current debts. We feel that you should consult an accountant as to what method is best for your business as you acquire substantial inventory.

Some of the terms listed above are from *Accounting, the Basis for Business Decisions*, Sixth Edition. Walter B. Meigs and Robert F. Meigs. McGraw-Hill Book Co.

# Chapter 8

# PRICING YOUR INVENTORY

Trying to sell an air conditioner to an Eskimo or a Rolls Royce to an unemployed person? What if the advertisement reads "Ice cream cone on sale for $100?" How many would you buy at that price? Not many unless you had lots of money or desperately needed one.

Since your gift baskets are not one of the necessities of life, except when the customer has to have one quickly because they forgot that special occasion, you will need to discern that fine line between making a good profit and pricing yourself out of existence.

Pricing your baskets to make a profit is what will ultimately keep you successfully in business. When pricing your gift baskets, remember that you must be flexible with the contents. Have a variety of items in mind so that you can make the basket fit the customer's pocketbook.

The retail price of your basket will depend on the cost of the basket, the cost of the items inside the basket, how much time it takes to build each basket, the trimmings, postage if it is to be mailed, and mileage and time if it is to be delivered locally. Then figure in your profit margin. Finally, you have arrived at the retail price to the customer. Quite simple — or is it?

There are many different theories on how to mark up your baskets to be competitive and maintain a profitable business. The following are traditional standard pricing systems for markups (the amount added to the cost to cover overhead and profit in arriving at the selling price) and establishing a profit objective.

| | |
|---|---|
| Keystoning = | Doubling the price of a product. Wholesale cost $34.50 x 2 = $69.00 retail cost. |
| Keystone + 20% = | Wholesale cost $34.50 x 2 = $69.00 + 20% = $82.80 retail cost. |
| Keystone + Labor = | Labor is what you charge hourly. If your time is worth $15/hour, retail cost would be $69.00 + $15.00 = $84.00. |

What works best for you is fine as long as you are consistent. The main consideration here is to be flexible in choosing a pricing system that works for you in order to be profitable in this business.

*"When buyers don't fall for prices, prices must fall for buyers."*
— Anonymous

When you purchase items at retail prices, your profit margin will be less because you cannot take the same markup as you would for items priced at wholesale without pricing your baskets out of the market. Focus on your best selling baskets and buy your inventory at wholesale prices whenever you can. Keep in mind that a custom-designed basket will cost more and therefore you should charge accordingly.

*"The value you place on your inventory is a crucial issue because it has a significant effect upon your profits. From a theoretical point of view, the cost of an item of inventory includes the invoice price, minus any discount, plus all expenditures necessary to place the article in the proper location and condition for sale. Among these additional incidental costs are import duties, transportation-in (shipping or freight costs to your location), storage, insurance of goods being shipped or stored, and costs of receiving and inspecting the goods."*
— Accounting, the Basics for Business Decisions

In pricing the baskets or basket items, any additional costs, such as shipping and insurance, should be added into your total price. Try to keep your transportation costs to a minimum by using the most economical carrier and packing methods.

When purchasing high-end items, such as crystal, silver, or china, you should price merchandise on its merits (rather than applying an average markup as on most goods). Feature these high-end items in your advertising.

The following example will show you how to cost out your merchandise, giving consideration to shipping charges and discounts. You purchase three-dozen night lights from Niebush Creations for $3.75 per light. Niebush Creations is located in the Napa Valley so there will be a $4.50 shipping charge to a certain location. There is no tax because you are buying wholesale. Assuming that you will prepay for this order, the company gives you a 2% discount. Pricing this item would go like this:

36 night lights at $3.75 each = $135.00 (minus 2% discount for prepaying or paying in cash which comes to $2.70)
Add $4.50 for freight charge.

$135.00
  -2.70 (discount)
$132.30
  +4.50 (shipping)
$136.80 = Total Charge for 36 night lights
$136.80 ÷ 36 = $3.80 (your cost per light)

When ordering from basket wholesalers, it is important to understand that you sometimes buy certain styles in "sets." Most often, they will be sold in sets of threes and fives. Baskets are nested inside from large to medium to small. The following formula is an essential tool to use when buying "sets" of baskets and especially when pricing them for sale.

Example: You order a particular style of basket. There are several columns on the form with the following headings:

(1) QUANTITY ORDERED
(2) ITEM NO.
(3) DESCRIPTION or STYLE
(4) UNIT PRICE, and
(5) AMOUNT

On this particular order under "Description," it says, "Set/3 Bamboo Picnic 8x9x13 natural." Under the "Price" column, it says "$7.50 for set." To determine your cost on each basket in the set, (in this case 3), do the following:

Assign a value or number for each size:

Small basket = 2

Medium basket = 3

Large basket = 4

Total = 9

Divide price of set ($7.50) by 9 to assign a value for use in pricing the baskets. Then multiply each numerical value assigned each basket size and you now have your cost per basket.

A $7.50 ÷ 9 = $.83.

Therefore,

B 2 x $.83 = $1.66 = Price of small basket (your cost)
C 3 x $.83 = $2.49 = Price of medium basket (your cost)
D 4 x $.83 = $3.32 = Price of large basket. (your cost)

To determine the retail price just multiply by 2.

When selecting baskets for your line, remember that customers like big, impressive baskets with price ranges from $35.00 - $50.00.

| Example of Pricing a Basket | |
|---|---|
| Basket | $5.00 |
| Book on cats | 4.50 |
| Cloth place mats (2) | 3.00 |
| Linen napkins (2) | 2.50 |
| Fabric decorative stuffed cat | 9.00 |
| Special gourmet dressing | 1.25 |
| Cappucino (gourmet instant) | 1.95 |
| Salsa mix | .25 |
| Potpourri | 4.25 |
| Cat card | 2.25 |
| Gourmet crackers | .60 |
| Liner | .07 |
| Filler or excelsior | .10 |
| Decor (Baby's breath and other items) | .60 |
| **Total** | **$35.07** |

To determine the price you will charge for this basket, multiply by 2 (markup is 100%) = $70.14. Add $5.00 to $10.00 for your labor and creativity. The price you will be selling the basket for is $75.50 to $80.50. You have "keystoned" the wholesale price of the basket plus the contents and also charged for your time and creative talent. Round off cents if possible as customers are trained to see the "$.50 or .95" ($15.50 or $49.95). If this method does not work well for you, try another.

## Pricing Ribbon

In order to determine how much to charge for the bow you make for your baskets, follow these steps:

$ How much is the price per yard? (Divide the total cost of ribbon roll by number of yards in the roll.)

$ Measure the bows as you make them to determine how many yards of ribbon you are using.

Keep track of how much time you have spent on making this bow (your labor).

$ How much do you charge for your labor by the hour?

Example: If you charge an hourly rate of $10 and it takes 4 minutes to make a bow, you should charge $.68 for labor. ($10 divided by 60 minutes comes to $.17 per minute; multiply $.17 x 4 (minutes) = $.68.)

$ Add the $.68 to the cost of the ribbon you used to arrive at your base cost.

$ Now you can mark it up just as you would the products in the basket.

## PRICE MARKUP WORKSHEET

| ITEM | UNIT COST | NO. OF UNITS | SUBTOTAL | MARKUP | TOTAL |
|---|---|---|---|---|---|
| BASKET OR ANY CONTAINER | 5.00 | 1 | 5.00 | 100% | 10.00 |
| SUPPLIES | | | | | |
| LINER | .08 | 1 | .08 | 100% | .16 |
| PEANUTS | .08 | 1 | .08 | 100% | .16 |
| EXCELSIOR | .20 | 1 | .20 | 100% | .40 |
| PRODUCT | | | | | |
| ALMONDS | .89 | 1 | .89 | 100% | 1.78 |
| CRACKERS | .99 | 1 | .99 | 100% | 1.98 |
| JAMS | 1.20 | 3 | 3.60 | 100% | 7.20 |
| SALSA MIX | 1.25 | 1 | 1.25 | 100% | 2.50 |
| NAPKINS | .99 | 2 | 1.98 | 100% | 3.96 |
| WINE GLASSES | .99 | 2 | 1.98 | 100% | 3.96 |
| GOURMET COOKIES | 1.85 | 1 | 1.85 | 100% | 3.70 |
| CAPPUCCINO | 1.94 | 1 | 1.94 | 100% | 3.88 |
| ENHANCEMENTS | | | | | |
| BOW | 1.20 | 1 | 1.20 | 100% | 2.40 |
| SILK FLOWERS | 2.20 | 2 | 4.40 | 100% | 8.80 |
| DRIED FLORALS | .50 | 1 | .50 | 100% | 1.00 |
| BALLOONS | | | | | |
| WRAP | | | | | |
| CELLOPHANE | .85 | 1 | .85 | 100% | 1.70 |
| FOIL | | | | | |
| SHRINK FILM | | | | | |
| OTHER DECOR | 2.75 stuffed bear | 1 | 2.75 | 100% | 5.50 |
| LABOR | | | | 20% | 11.82 |
| TOTAL | | | | | $70.90 |

*Example Markup Sheet*

Now that we have given you a fair idea on how to price your baskets, let us go to the next chapter and see how to make them.

# Chapter 9

# CREATING THE BASKETS

On your mark, get set — go! This is the part you've been waiting for. Here are some of the elements to be considered when creating and assembling a gift basket.

1. Theme

2. Basket or other container

3. Color harmony

4. Product packaging and coordination

5. Shape and design

6. Basket building techniques

7. Finishing touches/artful display

8. Wrapping (covered in Chapter 10)

## Theme

Determine the theme you'll be using. If you're stumped, refer to the list in Chapter 6. As we mentioned, general theme baskets revolve around a special occasion such as baby, birthday, wedding, anniversary, get-well, new home, retirement, bon voyage, etc. Other themes revolve around products, such as pasta, chocolate, health food (low cholesterol, vegetarian, low fat, etc.), oriental foods, Thai food, cajun/creole, Tex-Mex (Southwestern), fruit, cheese and other gourmet foods. There are romantic themes and sports themes, and they can all be mixed and matched to suit the time of the year and the customer.

## Basket or Other Container

Choose a basket or container that will display your merchandise most creatively, or fit into the particular theme. When designing a basket with a kitchen theme, choose a nice, deep, country style basket — much more appropriate than a glitzy, flamboyant container or decorative tray. Remember, a gift basket does not always have to be a basket. Use a hand-crafted wooden container, a nice platter, hat box, ice bucket, ceramic pasta bowl, colander, antique container, flower pot, teapot, hamper, cradle, urn, wagon, bucket, oriental tray, deli crate or a designer box to name a few. For the holidays use a wooden sleigh, a wicker reindeer, etc. A gift basket can be made from anything that will meet the needs of your customer. A large salad bowl filled with seasonings and other accoutrements works well. A large plastic bucket is perfect for a "Housewarming" basket with household detergents, sponges, a house plant, coloring books to keep the children occupied during the move, etc. Versatility is the name of the game.

## Color Harmony

Harmonizing the colors in your basket ties your entire package together and can make or break the overall effect. If this is an area that is not your forte, go to your local library and check out books on color. Take an art class at your local adult education center. An artist's color wheel will help. Find out how decorators are using colors. Look at home decorating magazines to get some ideas on which colors go well together. When personalizing a basket, find out the favorite colors of the recipient.

*"I like to weave the predominant color of an eye-catching product that will go into the basket with linen napkins and use a complementary color to coordinate for the added decoration, bow or embellishment."*
— Camille J. Anderson

Color coordinating products in the basket often means wrapping them up for a fashionable flair. Use gift wrap, tissue, gold or silver foil, shimmering cellophane, etc. to add color and pizazz. Wrapping many boxed items in the basket in gold foil wrap and using black ribbon adds a dramatic richness to the look. Use any attractive gift wrap to blend in your color theme. If your products are packaged creatively, leave them alone. However, by gift-wrapping and/or tying ribbon around those that are rather plain, you can enhance your basket 100 percent.

Take, for example, a can of oysters. The can could be boring, but by repeating the label's three colors, you create a striking basket. To add to the continuity, tie 1/4-inch to 1/2-inch black or red ribbon around a package or box of crackers and the soup bowl — immediately the whole basket looks fabulous.

# Product Packaging and Coordination

The food products you put in your baskets must be selected for good eating, and for eye appeal. The products should complement one another and add to the attractiveness of the total look. Packaging is important. As mentioned before, if one of the ingredients in the basket is rather drab in appearance, enhance it by gift wrapping or adding a ribbon.

Prepare basket contents to enhance their quality:

☐ Remove all price tags, non-essential labels and anything that detracts from the product.

☐ Attach decorative stickers to cover labels or stickers that won't peel off. There is a wonderful variety of these stickers at your local crafts store.

*"For example, I always have my fruit stickers on hand. They are great to attach to jar lids of some jams, marmalades, and jellies to give them an attractive look. I affix the fishing group stickers on canned products that need a flair, such as chili (especially for a man's basket — it definitely denotes a masculine quality)."*

— Camille J. Anderson

Add flair to products in a jar by dressing it up with a jar cover and tiny ribbon. Use some scraps of material you have on hand that coordinate with the other items in the basket. Take your pinking shears and cut a round circle large enough to hang over the top of the jar lid. Using a hot glue gun, put a dot of glue in the center of the material to affix on top of the jar. Tie thin ribbon or decorative cord around jar and make a small bow.

Wrap the products in colorful paper or fabric color-coordinated with the rest of the package. Wrap a bar of soap with fabric or just a nice lacy ribbon and bow.

Use decorative mini boxes, decorative bags or tins in assorted sizes and shapes. Beautifully wrapped products create an outstanding gift ensemble presentation.

Repackage leftover merchandise i.e., placing stationery in a romantically wrapped Victorian box — it definitely adds to the perceived value of the basket.

It is easier and more effective to select one main product and build around it than have a number of potential *stars* that end up fighting for the customer's attention. For example, when using a gardening theme, choose a live plant first. Arrange garden tools, gloves, watering can, seeds, herbs and apron attractively in the basket to complement entire design.

*"I usually select one unusual item to accent the basket. For example, a lovely sea shell, a duck, bird, butterfly or flower, etc. Anytime you add an eye-catching item you are upgrading the quality of your baskets and the price goes up accordingly."*

— Camille J. Anderson

## Napkin Folds to Add Pizazz

Create more artfully designed baskets by learning these unique napkin folds that will add flair and excitement to your basket.

Also, napkins enhance the perceived value of the basket. These few examples of napkin folds will also give you the know-how for enhancing an elegant table setting and will place you in the top league of the nation's best basket designers.

Napkins can create a very pleasing and dramatic effect in your basket design. For example, the Fan Fold and the Swirl Fold napkins look quite elegant in a crystal wine glass. Now visualize the added beauty of embellishing with a few sprigs of greenery, a rose, or baby's breath, as you add the final touches to your basket design.

For those napkins that will not be placed in a wine glass, or wrapped around other items, simply bore a hole in the basket filler to add creative dimension and a desired effect. Be creative in using napkin folds. There should be no limitation on your imagination when it comes to any part of basket designing.

*"The key to creative basket designing is unlocking your imagination and a no limit attitude about experimentation."*

Don L. Price

## Tips to Fold By

✦ Practice your napkin folds with a square (easier than rectangular) cloth napkin on a flat surface.

✦ Iron wrinkled napkins before you use a fold.

✦ Purchase napkins that have the same color intensity and pattern on both sides.

✦ After you have mastered these napkin folds, go to the library and check out books on advanced napkin folding.

*The Fan Fold*

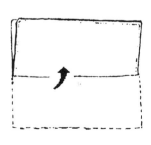

*Step 1. Fold in half.*

*Step 2. Fold into one inch accordion pleats.*

*Step 3. Position into wine glass and spread*

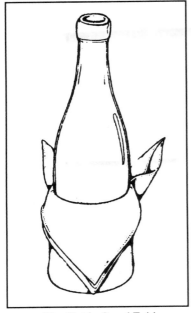

The Bottle Scarf Fold

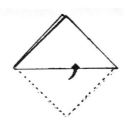

Step 1. Fold in half.

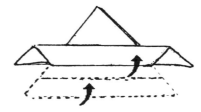

Step 2. Fold bottom edge up one quarter. Then again one more quarter.

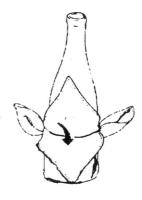

Step 3. Tie around the bottle. Then pull top down to the bottle.

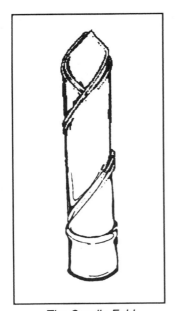

The Candle Fold

Step 1. Fold half corner to corner

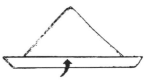

Step 2. Fold bottom edge up 1"

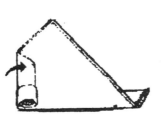

Step 3. Turn over and roll

Step 4. Tuck in corner and stand.

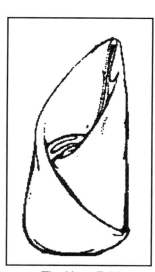

The Vase Fold

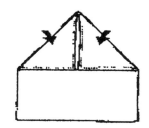

Step 1. Fold top corners to center

Step 2. Fold bottom half up

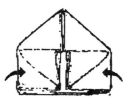

Step 3. Fold half down

Step 4. Fold sides to middle

Step 5. Fold in half and tuck in flap

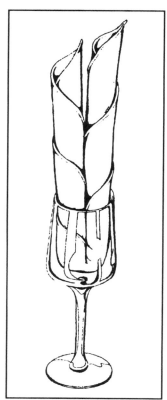

The Swirl Fold

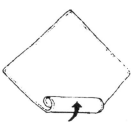

Step 1. Place flat and roll

Step 2. Bend and position into wine glass

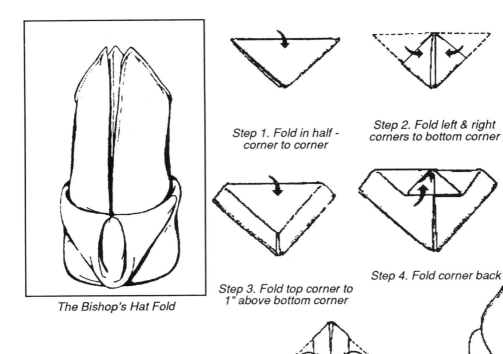

The Bishop's Hat Fold

Step 1. Fold in half - corner to corner

Step 2. Fold left & right corners to bottom corner

Step 3. Fold top corner to 1" above bottom corner

Step 4. Fold corner back

Step 5. Flip vertically for tight side up

Step 6. Fold back sides & tuck in back

Step 7. Turn down right & left corner points, and tuck

# Shape and Design of Basket

Like any work of art, your basket designs will have a distinct dimension in line, depth, balance, color and overall shape. Gift basket designing is similar to floral designing in that there are certain fundamental shapes most arrangements follow. The most basic gift basket shapes are:

☐ Round

☐ Triangular

☐ Oval

☐ Crescent shape

☐ The "S" curve.

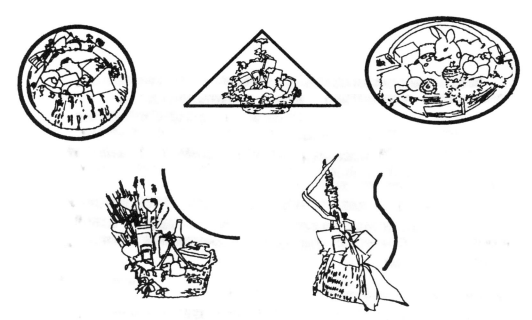

The overall effect of your basket is a critical factor in determining your success. Take a floral design class or browse through floral design books to acquaint yourself with basic design concepts. Make a statement with your design. Find a niche that makes your baskets stand out above your competition. Studies have shown that average sales will jump with a slick package design.

## Basket Building Techniques

The mechanics of constructing a gift basket are explained later in this chapter under "Assembling the Basket." Have all your supplies and tools on hand — basket liner, peanuts or crumpled paper, excelsior or other filler, ribbon, silks, scissors, wire cutters, floral wire, pipe cleaner, glue sticks, and hot glue gun. For upscale baskets, you will also need floral foam blocks for silk flowers, floral picks, floral u-pins and spanish moss.

## Finishing Touches/Artful Display

After examining your basket, products and embellishments, you will determine how you will place them in the container or basket. Refer to basket designs that have caught your attention in your magazine browsing. Go with the flow. If you are in a creative mood, let your imagination go wild! The visual expression of your finished product is so very important.

Enhance the beauty of your baskets with dried floral fillers such as eucalyptus, baby's breath, caspia, and German statice. These "fillers" are great for filling in empty spaces and add an airy look to your basket arrangement. Unusual items with an oriental flair such as a juniper sprig, cane cone, bleached twisted yanagi, tomaki, wisteria vine, etc.; or branches such as manzanita and birch look exotic in the overall basket design.

Try lotus pods, bell cup, palm cap and other distinctive pods on stems to create an element of excitement to the basket design. Beautiful grains such as black beard wheat, wild oats, cattails, and Indian broom add texture. Palms, such as the long stem palmetto, add a terrific backdrop to your basket and give it a dramatic look. Exquisite ferns, bamboo and ivy enhance the total look.

Silk florals such as bird of paradise, lilies, orchids, roses, daisies, and poinsettias at Christmas, look terrific and add color and flair. Potted plants and cactus accentuate any theme.

Your customer will be more attracted to a basket with foliage or floral design compared to a basket without. The baskets look bigger and this interprets to be more — which means a higher selling price.

Balloons are another way of enhancing your basket design and add that whimsical feeling. Mylar balloons are very popular with basket designers, but the regular balloons may be used for the same effect even though they don't last as long.

Craft merchandise is popular in baskets. There is a wave of consumer demand for unique, handmade products that are high in quality workmanship. Handmade items made in the United States are gaining in importance. Go to the library or craft stores to find creative ideas to place in your baskets.

*"One year I made decorative pomanders to place in my baskets. They exuded a wonderful scent and the recipients of the baskets were delighted to know they could hang this decoration in a closet or anywhere in their home to freshen the air! Another year, I made potpourri ornaments and ducks for Christmas. They were a hit! That was many years ago and these customers tell me that they bring them out every year at Christmas.*

*— Camille J. Anderson*

Stuffed animals in any form, from mysterious jungle animals to birds, ducks, geese, etc., are always a great way to add that special touch to the basket. A lion, tiger, monkey, giraffe or elephant nestled in appropriate foliage to create the feeling of the wild jungle, is a terrific way to add color, drama and beauty to your overall basket design.

For holiday baskets, spray pine cones with a clear glaze spray (purchased from any craft store) and then sprinkle glitter on them to add a lovely sparkle. Add a string of miniature, battery-operated lights to the basket handle and voila! — not only outstanding, but the price goes up.

Use lace, decorative trim and beads to create a gorgeous feminine effect.

Last, but not least, don't forget the beautiful bows you can make with the terrific selection of ribbons, both in color and design, available at a wholesale florist, craft store or through a catalog. All of the above mentioned finishing touches — that decorative flair — will set your baskets apart from all the others!

## Tying Up Profits

The exciting array of ribbons in bold, beautiful colors, designs and textures will add pizazz and flair — that finishing touch to your baskets. Some may think bow-making is difficult. However, after following these directions and with a little practice, you'll have this down to a science and no doubt will advance to becoming a bow-making expert!

## *Single Loop Bow*

**Step 1**

Cross ribbon in front. Bring back part to meet front.

**Step 2**

Pinch at center. Secure with #24, #26 or #28 gauge floral wire, twist and cut.

## *Multi-Looped Bow*

**Step 3**

Before you secure with wire continue from Step 2. Make third loop as shown, bringing ribbon behind, then up and over.

**Step 4**

Make fourth loop so ribbon is pointing down.

**Step 5**

Pinch in center. Secure with wire and twist ends together and cut. Trim ends of ribbon with an inverted "V" to give a finished look.

**Step 6**

Make fifth loop bringing ribbon on back side and then upward. Make sixth loop with ribbon aiming down front side. Pinch. Secure with wire in center and twist ends together. Leave enough ribbon for streamers.

**Step 7**

Make one more small loop and bring one end of wire back around and twist. Trim end of streamers by cutting inverted "V" to give a finished look.

## Assembling the Basket

1. Line basket with either plastic or cellophane or tissue paper (colored cellophane or tissue paper can tie into your color scheme).

*Figure 1*

As you assemble the contents for the basket, remember not to be skimpy. Make the basket look full or use a smaller container/basket. Your baskets should look delectable and should display as much merchandise as possible.

2. Put filler in the basket. If you are working with a larger, deep basket, you can use foam peanuts or crumpled craft paper, or crumple a brown paper bag and fill half of the basket.

*Figure 2*

3. Top off the basket with straw (excelsior), shredded paper, cellophane grass or waxed straw. Make sure that you have a firm foundation.

*Figure 3*

4. Have at least five to seven items attractively displayed and visible. Starting with the largest or tallest product bore or sculpt a pocket in the excelsior. Then wedge the product firmly into place. Place your larger products toward the back side of the basket, label facing forward, to form a support wall to keep the basket balanced. You do not want your ingredients to sink into the basket. They need to be propped up and artistically displayed.

*Figure 4*

5. Place the smaller, heavier products toward the front row of the basket. Sculpt these items into the excelsior at an angle so that they lean slightly back.

*Figure 5*

6. If needed, add more excelsior when you place the second row of products, usually lighter and smaller than the first row. You are actually sculpting a shelf for each product. See photo showing glassware strategically arranged in second row, bored into excelsior and slightly angled outward. Make sure the products sit up in the basket at an angle and do not disappear or sink into the straw.

*Figure 6*

7. Continue adding products using the lighter products as you work higher.

Note: If you are working with large baskets or other containers, remember to counterbalance the size and shape of products against each other. If using a shallow, elongated basket with a product such as sparkling cider, place another heavier item on the opposite end to prevent basket from tipping or sitting lopsided.

*Figure 7*

There are many techniques that gift basket designers use. Once you experiment with the basics, you will adopt your own style for sculpting and layering in the basket or container.

## Final Touches

8. After placing all the products in the basket, add your final touches. In this photo we trim the stem of a silk floral to fit the design and shape of basket.

*Figure 8*

9. Place silks into excelsior. In this photo, we also added a wooden duck for the final accent.

*Figure 9*

These adornments and final touches assure the final sale. They create visual appeal and promote your seasonal themes. Incorporate an element of whimsy — or a special keepsake that grabs the buyer's attention. Be creative and think about things that would make the basket fun. This will vary according to theme and style of the basket. In the fall and winter months, add a stem or two of eucalyptus with some sprigs of baby's breath. This gives the basket a total look and adds depth and texture.

During the holidays, place pine cones sporadically throughout the basket and embellish with a cluster of berries and pine. Artificial sprays of pine and berries, which look like the real thing, can be purchased from a wholesale florist or a craft store. Use fresh boughs of pine, Douglas fir, etc., to make your baskets come alive with Christmas. Use cinnamon sticks made up like a small "yulelog." The nostalgic scent of the holidays can be a hallmark of your baskets. Stay away from anything that looks too plastic or artificial.

In the spring and summer embellish the basket by adding a few silk stems such as daises, roses, etc., whatever ties in with your color theme. Ivy stems add a wonderful enhancement to the basket — you can work with them so they climb up and over the basket and trail in a very natural manner.

## Upscale Floral Designing

We have talked about the importance of using florals, foliage and other enhancements in the basket to add to the perceived value, therefore increasing profits. Almost always you will be adding one to three stems of a silk floral, foliage or exotic stem that can be poked directly into the excelsior without doing anything else (as shown above). Occasionally, your focus will be on the floral design as the main attraction of the basket. The basic technique is listed below:

1. Eyeball basket and determine where you will place the floral design and how you will place the other products in the basket to create a visually attractive and balanced product.

2. Take a floral foam block and cut it to the size you need by using a sharp serrated knife.

3. Take thin floral wire, place it around the foam block and attach to the bottom or side of the basket, depending upon configuration. Twist wire and snip off the excess. On occasion, sticky florist clay placed in strips on one side of the floral foam block will be enough to secure it to the base of the basket.

4. Place Spanish moss (purchased from a wholesale florist or craft store) over floral foam block and secure with florist u-shaped pins.

*Step 1.*

*Step 2.*

5. If stem is not sturdy enough to insert into the floral foam block, take a branch, florals, sprigs of ivy or other foliage and reinforce with wooden floral picks. If you need to add length to a stem, use #16 or #18 gauge floral wire and floral tape and secure by wrapping around stem, rolling and twirling tape with thumb

and forefinger while at the same time stretching tape as you move up on stem.

6. Insert stem deep into floral foam block.

7. Continue inserting florals into floral foam. Position flowers as if radiating to right and left. Remember, flowers are used in odd numbers. This is where the eye will focus.

8. Place foliage sprigs such as ivy on the edge and side of the floral foam block to create a natural look of trailing ivy flowing from the basket.

9. Now stand back and admire. You have just created a masterpiece!

*And Here's Your Finished Basket*

# Advance Basket Technique — The Pyramid

On occasion, you might want to dabble in a basket technique that takes more time and effort, but it will also warrant higher prices. You'll be glad to have this method under your belt.

Floral foam can be purchased in sheets or blocks. Cut to size and shape that will fit the basket like a glove.

☞ Wedge foam block into basket or container so you have a tight fit.

☞ Completely cover the foam block with decorative straw (color to match product) and anchor with floral u-pins (fern pins).

☞ Now wedge the smaller boxed products into foam block to create a shelf or let product rest on the edge of the basket supported by handle. Also, you can use long wooden floral picks (available through your local wholesale florist) inserted in foam to form support ledge.

☞ Take packaged product such as potpourri. Wrap wire of floral pick around neck and insert into foam.

☞ Continue to add products to the foam block by either wrapping suitable products with wire or wooden pick and inserting, or, building a ledge or shelf for product to rest on by inserting wooden picks into foam.

*The Finished Basket*

## Curling Ribbon on a Basket Handle

Curling ribbon on basket handle is an excellent way to add a different feeling to your basket design. Start at inside where handle meets basket. Dot hot glue and secure. Make a crinkle by giving slack in ribbon, then dot approximately every one inch to inch and one-half with hot glue to handle. Continue dotting and crinkling until entire handle is covered.

## Helpful Hints

* To use hot glue gun insert glue wax stick into base of gun. Heating element melts the glue. It dries quickly and is hot when ejected from glue gun so be extremely cautious and follow manufacturer's directions.

* If you will be creating lots of floral enhanced baskets, it might be wise to purchase a floral pick machine at your local wholesale florist for reinforcing stems to insert into floral foam.

* Silk florals are usually purchased with straight, stiff stems. To enhance your total design, bend and shape stem giving them a more natural look.

* When using filler such as baby's breath and German statice, break off sprigs where joint attaches on stalk. Shape into clusters. Wrap floral pick wire around stem. Secure with green floral tape.

These fillers can be added sporadically to basket to create an airy look and fill in those vacant spots.

* To wrap ribbon around handle of basket, dot hot glue on one end of ribbon and place inside of basket handle where handle meets rim. Wrap ribbon around handle, strategically spacing for overall basket design.

* Silk flowering plants, such as silk cyclamen, can be purchased from your local wholesale florist or craft store. These are wonderful to use in your basket design and you don't have to do any arranging. Cover foam block with Spanish moss. Insert entire thick base of plant into block. These foliage plants create a fantastic floral extravaganza.

Now that you have learned how to build the baskets, how do you package them for delivery?

# Chapter 10

# HOW TO WRAP, PACK AND SHIP

**H**ow should you present the final product? Should you leave the basket and ingredients to speak for themselves? Should you cellophane or shrink wrap the basket?

This is a question that only you can answer. One of the determining factors is whether it is for local delivery or mailing. If you are delivering locally, and the basket contents are secure, you can let the basket "speak for itself" with the contents in full display. However, sometimes you will get a request for wrapping with cellophane by the customer, or common sense tells you that the basket's ingredients will be more protected by cellophane or shrink wrap. When you are shipping, you must wrap the basket.

In the gift basket industry, professionals refer to cellophane wrapped baskets as "soft-wrapped." Other materials such as netting and chiffon can also be used for an elegant effect.

## *General Guidelines for Soft-Wrapping a Basket*

- ✂ You can purchase wide-width cellophane through floral and craft supply wholesalers.
- ✂ After assembling the basket, place it in the center of the cut and measured cellophane (you can approximate how much you need by "eyeballing" and doing some estimated measuring in your head). Gather cellophane up loosely

around the sides of the basket and squeeze at the top. Tie the cellophane with a decorative cord or ribbon. If you like a fanned, even effect, trim off cellophane in straight line across the top.

✂ You can buy colored cellophane. This adds a glowing effect around the holidays.

*I used red cellophane on a large corporate gift basket order which made the baskets look very festive and also held the contents well for delivery.*
Camille J. Anderson

## General Guidelines for Shrink Wrapping

Shrink wrap equipment (heat gun and shrink wrap) can be purchased through some craft stores, but mostly through manufacturers and wholesalers. (We have provided a list of companies that handle this equipment in the source section of this book.) Shrink wrap can be purchased in pre-made bags, or in various widths on a roll.

Some of the new concepts that have come on the market are called "shrinkable bags." There are varied and simple methods for using these shrinkable bags.

(1) Simply drop the bag over the product, placing the excess under the basket and shrink.

(2) Place the basket in the bag and fold the open end over, taping it closed, and presto — Shrink!

(3) Place the basket in the bag and seal with heat sealers.

Use whatever works best for you. Each manufacturer or supplier will provide instructions and suggestions on different techniques for shrink wrapping.

If you decide to use shrink wrap, a 250-foot roll wraps about 125 to 150 gift baskets (good and economical size to use). However, shrink wrap rolls are available in 100- to 2000-foot rolls. Shrink bags are available in sizes 18x18 inches up to 36x30 inches. A heat gun that shrinks the wrap is usually priced under $50. Do not use hair dryers because the voltage is too weak.

# Packaging and Shipping

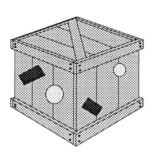

Shipping gift baskets is always a given when you handle corporate accounts and business or client gifts outside your immediate marketing area. As your business grows, your customers will require you to ship gift baskets all across the country.

If you have the time or the help, you can handle the shipping yourself. You can assemble and package the baskets in preparation for shipping and mail through your chosen carrier.

*Because we were so busy during the holiday rush and were blessed with so many orders out of our targeted marketing area, we decided to take the gift baskets to a "Packaging Outlet." They became well acquainted with us and our product and handled the packaging and shipping of the gift baskets with expert care.*

We suggest that if you decide to use a packaging outlet, first check several for reliability, then take sample sizes in to have them weighed. The outlet can cost out each basket factoring in the destination charges for you. With this information, you can price the baskets accordingly. Even though you will have to add in the extra cost for packaging and shipping, your clients will be assured of their gifts arriving on time and undamaged.

You may find that as your business grows, it will be more cost effective to package and ship the baskets yourself using an overnight delivery service to pick up at your place of business. If this is the case, plan for extra help and have all packaging materials on hand.

Pay particular attention to the strict requirements the carriers have on weight and measurements (size of the container). Make sure your containers are sturdy, and check for the strength and grade on the containers you use. When packing, go the extra step by layering the bottom of the box, all sides, and the top using shredded or rolled newspaper and/or plastic bubbles.

## How to Prepare Your Baskets for Shipping

When you assemble your baskets, think snug, tight, and secure. Placing enough filler in the basket is the first key for ensuring that your basket products are held securely in place and therefore received by the customer in one piece.

Techniques for assembling your baskets for packaging and shipping:

☛ Use tape, wire, floral sticks, and a hot glue gun to help secure products when constructing your baskets.

☛ Keep breakable items separate so they do not touch each other. You can use tissue paper to tuck around glass or similar decorative material to protect the basket products.

☛ Use cellophane wrap to completely cover the basket and tie a bow at the top, or

☛ If you have shrink wrap tools, shrink wrapping is the best way to secure the products in the basket to facilitate boxing and shipping.

## Tools You Will Need

When you begin handling multiple orders that require shipping, be prepared. The following tools are essential:

Shipping containers — most shipping services have specially designed envelopes, boxes and tubes available to you at no cost. These containers work well when shipping smaller items.

• Tape dispensers — hand-held or pull-handle

• Rolls of mailing tape

• Packaging materials — shredded newspaper, brown paper bags (save those grocery bags), bubble sheets, polystyrene "peanuts," shredding, recycled packaging material

• Shipping labels — printed with Perishable, Fragile, etc.

• Weighing scale up to 80 pounds

## Shipping Services

There are a number of shipping services available that offer both surface and air freight shipping. They offer next-day delivery, standard or next-day air from door to door, from airport, from airport baggage counter to destination airport baggage counter, post office to post office, post office to addressee, and railroad station to railroad station. As you become more familiar with the various shipping services and their delivery benefits, you will be better able to select the ones that service your needs best. Some carriers offer quantity discounts for volume shipping. Others offer excellent same-day or next-day service. Some deliver on weekends, while others deliver only on Monday through Friday. Still others can offer worldwide service.

Be selective and compare each company's service guides carefully and study the fine print. Test the reliability of the carriers you select. Send two similar packages with two different carriers to the same location to ascertain which gives the best quality of service for the price.

Make sure you consider the following things when shipping baskets:

1. Any basket with perishable foodstuff must be marked.

2. Mark baskets that contain breakable items.

3. Do not tie the outer package with string or use anything other than heavy duty packing tape to secure the box.

4. Comply with the carrier's address labeling on the box for proper delivery.

If you set up your business for delivery service, call the carriers in your area and ask them to send you their service guide. For example, if UPS is selected as one of your carriers, the local representative will provide you with an introductory "Customer Materials Kit" full of explanatory guidelines and the various payment options available. You will also receive materials such as a shipper number stamp, record log and measurement chain. They assign a daily pickup time and route carrier.

If you decide on using DHL Worldwide Express, they will have a delivery service representative drop off their Quick Reference Guide to explain service/packaging, invoicing, transit times, destinations, international document rates/package rates and domestic rates.

## *List of Carriers*

The following is a list of possible shipping companies. Check your telephone directory for those available in your area.

---

Parcel Post — U.S. Post Office-to-door delivery

United Parcel Service (UPS) — Door-to-door service

DHL Worldwide Express — Door-to-door service

Federal Express — Door-to-door service

Amtrack Package Express — Railroad station to railroad station

Intercity and Interstate Bus Lines — Bus terminal to bus terminal

Independent Motor Freight Lines — Door-to-door service

Priority Mail — U.S. Post Office — Post office-to-addressee service

Express Mail (U.S. Post Office) — Post office to addressee service

Airline Small Package Service — Airline baggage counter to airline destination baggage counter

Air Freight Service Companies — Door-to-door service

---

The next chapter will cover personal deliveries.

# Chapter 11

THOSE BLOOMIN' BASKETS, ETC.

# MAKING THE DELIVERIES

To save time and wear and tear on you and your car, arrange your deliveries in a logical order so that you are not running all over town needlessly. Devise a delivery system that fits into a time frame that is convenient for you and your customers.

Delivering your gift baskets is fun. It might even be the high point of your day — a chance to meet new people, see how they live, learn about new things, make new contacts, and gather fresh ideas for your baskets.

Here are some tips to save time:

- ☛ Mark zip codes on a good city map and plot out your route to prevent backtracking or going out of your way.
- ☛ As baskets are prepared, you can color code them for designated delivery routes.
- ☛ Group these color coded baskets to expedite delivery.
- ☛ If possible, set up temporary storage space with the baskets color coded and grouped according to the route. This enables the designated delivery person to load baskets on their own without having to interrupt your work.
- ☛ Invent unique costumes to wear when delivering your baskets. Wear a tuxedo for romantic or formal occasions; and maybe, a bunny outfit for Easter deliveries. If delivering to a children's hospital, dress in a clown or cartoon character costume. For marketing value you can have shirts

printed with your business name and logo. Wear something that is snappy, sharp and will leave a lasting impression with your customer.

☛ Determine delivery fees according to area. You can charge anywhere from $2 - $10 depending on the distance and time involved.

☛ If you are delivering to a military base, get information on their gate policies. For instance, do you need a special clearance or pass to get in? Do you leave the basket at the front gate or Visitor Center? Get this information before you leave the house.

☛ When you have a large order to deliver at one location, i.e., an office building in the downtown area, it is a good idea to have a companion with you to expedite the delivery process and sometimes avoid parking meters and related expense. The driver can circle the block while you are delivering.

☛ If you have several large orders for special holidays and have planned to use more than one driver, assemble a "car caddy" for each driver to include:

1. A city map

2. A coin purse with change for meter, parking, telephone, gas and meals

3. Writing tools

4. A mileage and delivery log

5. Name and number of towing company you use

☛ Remember to keep your mileage log up-to-date. Record beginning and ending odometer reading for tax purposes.

**Chapter 12**

# $A$DVERTISING AND PROMOTION

*"Doing business without advertising is like winking at a girl in the dark. You know what you're doing but no one else does."*

— Stewart H. Britt

$A$dvertising, as defined by Webster, is "Printed or spoken matter that advertises; advertise; to tell about or praise a product, service, etc. publicly, as through newspapers, handbills, radio, etc., so as to make people want to buy it."

Marketing, as defined by Webster, is "All business activity involved in the moving of goods from the producer to the consumer, including selling, advertising, packaging, etc."

So now that you know what these two words mean, how do you go about implementing them in your business? Let's begin with different strategies of how and where to promote your business (marketing) and, at the same time, how to incorporate advertising into moving goods from you, the producer, to the consumer.

In marketing and promoting your Specialty Gift Basket Business, you'll come across many profitable and creative ways to increase sales. The idea is to always be open and flexible to new and innovative concepts with which to increase and build your business. We have listed several marketing approaches to promote your business. They have proven to be highly successful for many in this industry.

## Home Parties

Tupperware, crystal, jewelry, sexy lingerie — and now gift baskets have joined the ranks of the ever popular Home Party. Home parties are a terrific way to introduce friends, relatives and associates to your new business. You can start out by inviting a few friends and relatives to your home for an introduction to your basket line. Have an order form available for each guest. Describe each one of your gift baskets, the material, type of weave, where it is from, the theme it represents, and the contents. Of course, this is a good time to suggest ways the basket can be used in the future, both functionally and decoratively. Being in your own home the first time you hold a basket party will help you maintain control and be more relaxed. Enjoy yourself and see how many baskets you sell your first time out.

ORDER FORM

THOSE BLOOMIN BASKETS

Name: _____  Date: _____
Address: _____  Zip Code: _____
Phone No. (Day) _____  Evening: _____

| QUAN. | ITEM NO. | DESCRIPTION (State color preference where essential) | PRICE | AMOUNT |
|---|---|---|---|---|
| | 011 | Deluxe Pasta Basket | $ 68.95 | |
| | 012 | Standard Pasta Basket | 48.95 | |
| | 013 | Picnic Basket (Yellow, red, blue & brown) | 49.95 | |
| | 014 | Deluxe Kitchen Basket | 54.95 | |
| | 015 | Pine Cone Dried Floral Spray | 39.95 | |
| | 016 | Sport's Basket (Tennis, Golf or whatever) | 45.95 | |
| | 017 | Indoor Gardening Basket | 37.95 | |
| | 018 | Jug Vase Dried Floral Spray | 35.95 | |
| | 019 | Gourmet Wine & Cheese Basket | 24.95 | |
| | 020 | Bathroom Basket | 24.95 | |
| | 021 | Deluxe Bar Ensemble (Hen Basket) | 22.95 | |
| | 022A | Hen Basket-Preserved Roll Centerpiece (kitchen towel) | 18.95 | |
| | 022B | Hen Basket-Preserved Roll Centerpiece (filling) | 18.95 | |
| | 023 | Hanging Doll Cradle (with Johnson gift set) | 19.35 | |
| | 024A | Hanging Doll Cradle (floral display with baby) | 14.95 | |
| | 024B | Hanging Doll Cradle (floral display only) | 12.95 | |
| | 025 | Owl- Dried Floral Spray | 8.50 | |
| | 026 | Elephant - Dried Floral Spray | 8.50 | |
| | 027 | Elephant - Dried Floral Spray (wood-tone) | 8.50 | |
| | 028 | Owl- Felt-tip Pen Gift Basket | 8.95 | |
| | 029 | Owl - Mini Tool Set Gift Basket | 8.95 | |
| | 030 | Elephant - Incense Gift Basket | 8.50 | |
| | 031 | Owl - Screwdriver Gift Basket | 8.50 | |
| | 032 | Hen Basket with Dried Floral Arrangement | 24.95 | |
| Please specify special order below: | | | TAX | |
| | | | TOTAL | |

*Have Your Order Forms Ready*

*At the very first basket party given by Those Bloomin' Baskets, etc., we introduced our product line to a group of friends and associates, and made a whopping $500.*

Be organized and get your invitations in the mail at least two weeks in advance. Serve hors d'oeuvres and beverages to add to the party atmosphere. After you make your presentation, ask who would be interested in hostessing the next basket party at their home. If a hostess can gather a group of about 20 friends and family, you can offer her a gift basket — the size and type will depend on sales made at her gift basket presentation party.

Sometimes it helps to set up the deliveries on a one-time basis at the hostess's home. This can build your customer base rapidly.

## How To Make Contacts and Build a Customer List

Through your city's Chamber of Commerce, you can set up speaking engagements or basket parties using their contact lists. Also, if speaking publicly is your forte, set up presentations with other professional groups and service organizations such as Toastmasters and women's clubs. Use your personal contacts such as your physician, dentist, nail and hair salon, gym, club, bank, and others you deal with. Always have your business cards with you and carry a portfolio or small photo album that displays the uniqueness and quality of your baskets.

Keep your product visible by taking a small, but impressive basket to your hairdresser, for instance, and say "thank you" for her good service. Leave your business cards next to the gift basket. Other customers will definitely pay attention. Another good idea is to make up special small gift baskets or arrangements that can be placed at each teller station in your bank with your enclosure card and tags attached.

*Those Bloomin' Baskets, etc. decorated the bank where we opened our business account. They were thrilled to have the "gratis" decorative baskets that embellished the decor of the bank and it also helped us advertise our business. Every customer that came into that bank was exposed to the baskets and could take a business card if they were interested.*

## Consignments

Consignment means merchandise is placed in a shop and you are paid as the product sells. Hospital gift shops are a good place for arranging a consignment contract.

Putting your gift baskets on consignment is an excellent way of selling your baskets, and also making your business very visible. Call the Chamber of Commerce in your area to get the name and addresses of shops in your community, or "let your fingers do the walking through the Yellow Pages." You usually arrange to pay a commission contingent on the sales of your product.

The following tips will help the consignment choice work.

* Call the shops and pre-qualify them. Find out what merchandise they carry.

* Provide the store with a letter of introduction.

* Provide photographs of baskets displayed in a quality-bound portfolio.

* Be prepared to provide sample gift baskets on request.

## Selling Through Colleges

Find out if the colleges in your area send out printed material, i.e., a newsletter to the parents of the students. If so, place an ad in the newsletter. Help mom and dad out. Surprise their son or daughter with a care package or birthday present. It is a real boost to receive a basket of goodies during mid-term exams and finals.

## Trade Shows & Exhibits

Buy or share a booth at a trade show. Set up an attractive booth with props and a backdrop to display your gift baskets. You can request listings of trade events from local convention centers. Get acquainted with the business organizations in your community and participate in sidewalk sales, street fairs, and other promotional efforts that would be advantageous to your business.

When renting a booth at Home Shows that are open to the public in your area, experiment with several incentive ideas. For example, offer a discount card to people who stop and show interest (a 15%-20%

discount is attractive). The discount should expire after the next major holiday.

For greater exposure and selling potential, rent a kiosk or push-cart in a mall. The fee for kiosks is usually calculated per square footage plus a percentage of weekly gross sales. If renting for a special holiday, such as Valentine's Day (1-2 weeks), try to convince the mall management to waive the percentage fee. Have plenty of brochures to pass out and stage a drawing so that you can get customers to sign up with their name and address. This will build your mailing list.

## Craft Fairs

Participate in local craft fairs to expose your products.

*During the second year we were in business, I was asked to participate in a very prestigious event called "Christmas in the Country." Artisans from all over the area vie to display their wares at this event held at the distinctive Domaine Chandon (maker of fine champagne and wine) located in the Napa Valley. We were honored by this privileged invitation. It was an evening event and all the vintners, locals from the area, and residents from the San Francisco Bay Area attended.*

*Our Booth at Domaine Chandon*

*We spent a great deal of time designing the display to present our baskets and ornaments (as we were allotted only so many square feet). With the help of some wonderful friends, we came up with a terrific display and the gift baskets were a hit — so much so that*

*Those Bloomin' Baskets, etc. was asked back the next year. It was wonderful and needless to say, this definitely exposed the business threefold!*

## Co-ops

Cooperative marketing helps a small business get started by sharing operating costs while earning profits.

Co-ops are rented spaces (stalls, booths, etc.) within one large space, such as an old barn, refurbished house, warehouse, or storefront, where each participating business may display their goods. Vendors rotate their working schedules, share rent, advertising costs, utilities and insurance. Items sold are recorded, totaled and reimbursed to the vendors at a given time.

## Publicity

If your business provides a select and unique product and service, the media usually is interested in doing a feature newspaper or magazine article. This type of publicity is not only free advertising, but because it is written by a professional, it gives your business added recognition. Take advantage of it whenever you have the opportunity. You can call the local television, radio station or newspaper in your community and ask if they would be interested in doing a feature article on your particular subject. Give them a reason to be interested. Let them know that your specialty gift baskets are high-quality and that you customize your baskets to suit the needs of the recipient.

*We were fortunate in this area. The first year in business, we received a call from a local magazine that wanted to do a feature article on Those Bloomin' Baskets, etc. because they thought it was so unique. It was free advertising for us and gave the business great exposure. They even photographed an Easter Basket that was designed especially for their April issue. This magazine was very new and they featured businesses and restaurants that were germane to the area. We saved several copies of the magazine and used the article for the promotional and the credibility backing of our gift basket business. Twelve years later, this particular magazine (Sacramento Magazine) is one of the hottest selling magazines in the city.*

## Selling to Industries and Corporations

Search out approachable industries in your area and leave a few brochures with the Publicity, Public Relations, Marketing, and Personnel (Human Resources) Departments. If you speak with the receptionist, tell him/her you would like to make an appointment with the person in the company responsible for handling "Promotional Gift Ideas." Follow up, as busy executives appreciate having their gift giving taken care of with a phone call.

## Selling to Hotels

Amenity baskets are big with hotels. Baskets are given to special guests, such as, presidents, officers and executives of businesses and associations. They send baskets to meeting planners and organizers. Many hotels will contract with outside vendors, so make sure you pursue this market.

## Other Firms and Businesses to Approach

Try government offices, museum and art affiliations, real estate offices, printing companies, interior decorators, mall offices, insurance companies, construction firms, car dealerships, boat and yacht dealerships, architects, appraisers, accountants, spa resorts, golf and tennis clubs, medical facilities, and dental offices.

Real estate firms like to send unique gift baskets to new homeowners in appreciation for their business. This also exposes your business to the new homeowner.

*One of our customers bought gift baskets consecutively for three years for holiday client "thank yous." He is a prominent auto dealership owner and advertises heavily on television and in newspapers, which is why we pursued this account.*

*Each year we would present a totally new and unique basket in the budget range he allotted. Again, it was a challenge to create unique items that would catch his attention. We had a professional portfolio with photos and prices just for this firm. Samples of the baskets were always presented to him so he knew what his clients would be receiving. He realized that they would think of his auto dealership every time they smelled the aroma of the coffee or enjoyed the other goodies in the basket. Long after it was empty the unique basket itself would be a reminder.*

Golf clubs and country clubs offer a great opportunity for possible accounts. As an example, we landed a great account with a ladies' golf group at a very prestigious country club by writing a letter introducing the business. You can use it as a guideline.

```
                    THOSE BLOOMIN' BASKETS



                                          February 1, 1984

     Members of the
     Ladies' Golf Group


     Dear Members:

          I would like to take this opportunity to share with you
     a gift concept that I feel would be an exciting and innovative
     asset for your club tournaments.

          To begin with, my business, "Those Bloomin' Baskets"
     has been in operation for about 2½ years.  It offers a flair
     and quality in gift basket concepts and decor that are avant-
     garde.  I do take pride in my work and the authenticity of my
     gift-packaging concepts.  They are distinctive, dramatic,
     elegant, yet keenly discriminating--gifts and decor that are
     appealing to males and females of all age groups.

          At this time I am most interested in the possibility of
     getting involved in club tournaments whereby I would provide
     "x" number of baskets as "tournament" gifts or "tee-off" gifts
     or whatever, for your scheduled tournaments during the year.
     Because of the diversity of the line and constantly-flowing
     creative ideas that lend themselves to the "custom-designed"
     baskets, I could offer your group gift baskets that would be
     appropriate with inscriptions of sorts using Del Paso or any
     other name or logo you wish.  In other words, the choices that
     you ladies have are ad infinitum.

          To give you a brief background about my credibility,
     I would like to mention that I have had tremendous response to
     my basket line.  At the present, I am selling to a very special-
     ized market in Lake Tahoe, the Napa Valley (my baskets are being
     displayed in the elegant wine-tasting room of Sterling Vineyards
     and also for sale in their gift area).  At Beringers, above St.
     Helena, I have decorated their main room and gift area with my
     baskets and silks and do so on a seasonal basis.  I have also
     sold to a few establishments in the outlying areas of Carmel
     Valley, including Pebble Beach.  Furthermore, I am doing some
     free-lancing in silk flower design in conjunction with an
     interior decorator from Marin County and a developer of time-
     share condominiums at Lake Tahoe.  At the Americana Inn, I have
     decorated every unit with my baskets for centerpiece decor.
```

LADIES GOLF GROUP                -2-                    February 1, 1984

    In addition, this past fall, and also during the Holidays, I had the pleasure of doing business with Mr. Chuck Swift of Swift Dodge. He placed two substantial orders-- one for his 1984 new car promotion and the second, gifts for a long list of clients he deals with in Sacramento. They consisted of four different themes: Wine basket; Gourmet Pasta Basket; Nut and Condiment Basket; and Jam and Biscuit Basket. For his Christmas order, I provided him with the following: (1) silk-blend poinsettias in vine basket, (2) special fabric duck (with unique blend of fabric and colors) in vine basket, with handle embellished with fresh boughs of Christmas greenery, pine cones, nuts, etc.; Pine cone/apple/nut basket permanent centerpieces; and Grapevine wreaths with exquisite decor. One of my trademarks is to embellish my baskets with babys' breath and other dried flowers, silks, or whatever is appropriate for the season--to add that look of uniqueness and distinction.

    I would be happy to provide you with a list of references if you so desire of the various people I have worked with since the inception of my business--one of them being Mr. Bud Brody of Lake Merced Golf and Country Club. He is quite familiar with my baskets for golf tournaments.

    I am enclosing various items for your viewing: First, I have included some photographs from my line (including some of the baskets from Chuck Swifts order), exemplifying the quality and craftsmanship of my work. Second, I am enclosing the April issue of Sacramento Magazine containing an article about my basket business. Third, I have included some business cards for you to disperse to interested parties.

    It would be very easy for me to work around the golf theme and at some point in time, I could provide you with specific examples. I am also expanding my line in the spring to include gourmet specialty foods to appeal to those with gourmet palates.

    Ladies, thank you so much for taking the time to read about "Those Bloomin' Baskets." I would be most interested in showing you my portfolios at a time that is convenient for you. I do hope that my letter reaches you in a timely fashion for golf tournaments this year.

    Please feel free to contact m                758.

Encs.                                    Respectfully yours,

                              Camille Loo Smith
                              THOSE BLOOMIN' BASKETS

## Displaying at Business and Commercial Gatherings

Try to have a display of your baskets at any special event such as a new bank opening, open house, car dealership promo, or wine-tasting event. Be aware of special events for organizations and clubs, i.e., a garden club luncheon, church bazaar or fund raiser. Present the idea of using gift baskets for table centerpieces.

*We secured a nice account with the Women's Legal Auxiliary in our area. They were looking for centerpieces to adorn the tables at the Red Lion where they were having a special luncheon featuring the infamous critic of women's fashions — Mr. Blackwell. They had a budget of $15 per centerpiece. It was a challenge to work within their budget and come up with something unique and colorful. There were*

100 tables that sat ten people each. It was worth the effort for the exposure. We managed to come up with a unique basket centerpiece that tied in with Mr. Blackwell's personality.

We purchased 100 cut mirror tiles and attached floral foam blocks with a hot glue gun to the mirror. The foam block was wrapped with black, shiny, quality ribbon. A red bow tie was affixed to the wrapped foam block. Emerging from the center was a crystallized, decorative, birch branch and three red silk roses. A colorful butterfly was attached to the birch branch. It was a hit. The exposure to so many women was terrific and the profits from that order were great.

## Holiday Open House

Have a "Holiday Happening" either in your own home or in a rented room at a popular restaurant in your area. Having an "Open House" or "Wine and Cheese Basket Party" is a great way to introduce your business to relatives, friends, and their friends, and business contacts.

If you hold this event at a restaurant, you will probably attract some of the restaurant patrons as well. The general public loves unique gifts and therefore your baskets will be a hit. Before the holidays, people are desperate to find appropriate gifts and don't have the time to shop. That's why you are there — to take care of their gift-giving needs. Make it an elegant affair. Offer hors d'oeuvres, champagne and wine. Set a festive, holiday mood with the proper lighting, decor and displays. Your customers will love to browse, eat, drink and buy.

If you decide to hold this holiday event in your home, you might want to offer a special holiday mulled wine (mix) that you are featuring in your gift baskets. Not only does it emanate the "feeling" of the holidays, it also promotes your baskets. Another good idea is to warm simmering potpourri on your stove or in the containers that the potpourri comes with. Your entire home will be filled with the holiday spirit in every sense of the word. Make sure you use a scent such as berry, pine, cinnamon, or cloves.

*Our holiday open houses became one of the big "events of the season." Invitations were sent to businesses, friends, and acquaintances; everyone attended. All the gift baskets were strategically set up around the house, along with handmade Christmas ornaments. We served hors d'oeuvres, holiday drinks, cookies, and other goodies. Everyone thoroughly enjoyed themselves and were in no hurry to go home. Happily, many baskets and ornaments were bought at this holiday open house.*

*A special "wrap" room was set up with my daughter being "Number One Gift Wrap Girl." She did a beautiful job and my customers left feeling good about their purchases. It was a profitable evening for all of us. My guests were able to shop and enjoy a holiday social event at the same time.*

This event has become a tradition, and each year people ask if there will be another "Holiday Open House."

## Bridal Market

Promote your wedding selections' versatility. Let your customer know that gift baskets are not for just the bridal shower and wedding gifts. Tell them they can be used as thank yous to be delivered after the wedding to the parents, in-laws, pastor and wedding party. You might also suggest small baskets as "tokens of appreciation" to greet out-of-town relatives at their hotel room. You might even consider having a special brochure detailing the bridal package.

To promote your wedding gift basket package, contact bridal salons in your area and tell them about your services. Leave your card. Find out about bridal fashion shows in your area through the Chamber of Commerce. You can participate in local bridal seminars or adult community courses on wedding preparations to expand your clientele.

## Fund Raisers

Fund raisers can be a terrific way to expose your baskets. Select the charities or organizations you wish to target and present them with your gift basket ideas. They can be used as table decor and for gift drawings or prizes. Show them your brochure and portfolio so they can see the quality of your baskets. Each basket the charity sells earns a commission, and this is a good way to have the name of your business imprinted in the minds of the recipients.

*The high school our daughter attended always had one large function each year — a Crab Feed — and they asked me to donate a basket. Of course the answer was "yes." The name of our business was listed in the program and mentioned when they auctioned the donated gifts. It was great exposure as there was always a large attendance of fairly affluent parents, many of them community leaders and business owners in the area. I would donate a gift basket priced around $100 each year and it came back in measurable profits with added business down the road.*

## Subcontracting

Subcontract your gift basket services to specialty shops, department stores, sporting goods stores, gift shops, stationery stores, bookstores, bath and linen shops, restaurants, plant shops, china and collectible shops, etc. When you subcontract your services to create gift baskets for these retail stores, remember that you are promoting your work with their name on the basket. However, it is a way of creating sales for your business and definitely promotes the concept of gift baskets. Working in this capacity, you are actually a gift basket consultant. You can work on their premises or wherever they would prefer. In your sales presentation to get these accounts, tell them that you are a professional in the art of creating specialty gift baskets. You need to let them know that you can work faster and with better results than their current employees who have no experience in this area.

If you decide to go this route, you need to draw up a contract and *get everything in writing*. They may want you to do demonstrations in their store as customers browse and buy. There are many arrangements you can work out, such as a flat fee for your labor and packaging supplies while they supply the baskets and ingredients. Maybe they have a kiosk where you could operate and sell your own baskets, giving the store a percentage of your gross sales. Whatever arrangement you work out, investigate all possibilities and figure out on paper how the profits come out for you. It would be advisable to consult an attorney to draft the general contract letters.

## Word-of-mouth

One of your best marketing promotions is word-of-mouth. Once you have created baskets for customers and they like it, they will spread the word.

*"He who has a thing to sell! And goes and whispers in a well is not so apt to get the dollars. As he who climbs a tree and hollers."*

— Anonymous

## Join a National Membership Association

Consider joining an association that has state and local chapters. The benefits are:

- The name of your business is placed in a directory to which participating corporations subscribe.

- They send out quarterly fliers to corporations giving you an an excellent opportunity to promote special holiday baskets.

- They have vendor shows where the marketing representative visits certain corporations to display their products (local chapter).

- Monthly exchanges are another benefit. Hire a representative; they make a commission off what they sell. With gift baskets, around 15% is the going rate.

## Selling Wholesale to Other Retail Outlets

Many boutiques, gardening shops, and other specialty stores prefer to buy a line of gift baskets without all the headaches of assembling gift baskets for their store. This presents an opportunity for you to create a standard line of baskets that will give you a steady flow of business all year long. Keep in mind that your profit margin is smaller selling on a wholesale basis. However, having volume sales may be worth the effort. When selling wholesale, it is advisable to:

- Have purchase order forms either stamped, typed, or printed with the name of your business.

- Be prepared to show your baskets. The buyer wants to see the quality of your gift baskets.

- After you write an order, make sure you get a signed purchase order.

- Give the store its copy.

- Have the terms and conditions of the sales in writing and go over them with the client. Specify payment on delivery or 30 days from delivery date.

- Change prices twice a year (usually spring and fall).

- Notify customers immediately of price increases.

## Bureau of Tourism

Write to the Bureau of Tourism in your state to acquire ideas for your theme baskets. Find out activities and products indigenous to your area. Complement this aspect through gift basket designs.

## A Note about Mail Order

The mail order business is a whole new avenue that you as a gift basket specialty owner can pursue. It can be extremely profitable and fun. Instead of going into infinite detail on this facet of the business, we recommend that you obtain the brochure entitled *A Business Guide to the Federal Trade Commission's MAIL ORDER RULE* for sale by the Superintendent of Documents, U.S. Government Printing Office, Washington DC 20402.

# Advertising

*"Many a small thing has been made large by the right kind of advertising."*
— Mark Twain

In this section, we discuss ways to successfully advertise and create brochures and other advertising material.

In advertising your business, you'll soon realize that you have many options to exercise. You will find that the best advertising methods are those of happy clients who love to tell their friends about the beautiful baskets you created for them. However, in optimistic terms, there's the reality that to have a growing business year after year you will need to plan out a well executed advertising campaign using various forms of advertising. In the beginning you may have a limited budget and advertising experience. Therefore, many of the ideas that are listed will allow you to get maximum exposure as quickly as possible.

## Brochures

An eye-catching and effective sales brochure is imperative to attract your customers. Whether you choose to create a brochure yourself or have it done, there are certain guidelines that should be followed:

1. If it is to be mailed, it should fit into a business envelope.

2. If used as a "handout" (to medical offices, for example) 8 1/2- by 11-inch paper can be used to hang on bulletin boards.

3. If using a trifold (3 panel), the front cover must entice your customers to read inside.

a. Use a nice basket design logo or drawing along with the name of your business; or

b. Because baskets are so photogenic, use an actual photograph to add depth and drama to your message. You can have one large headline accompanied by a single photograph or a series of photos of equal size in a collage arrangement.

4. Tie pages together and keep the continuity of your brochure throughout by a heavy horizontal line that extends across the top of all three panels.

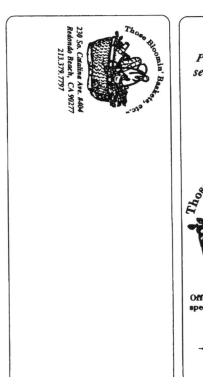

*Example of Three-Way-Fold Brochure*

5. Inside the brochure organize your information around visual elements such as color photographs or illustrations of your bas-

kets. Add a catchy title to immediately capture the attention of your potential customers and spark their interest to make a purchase.

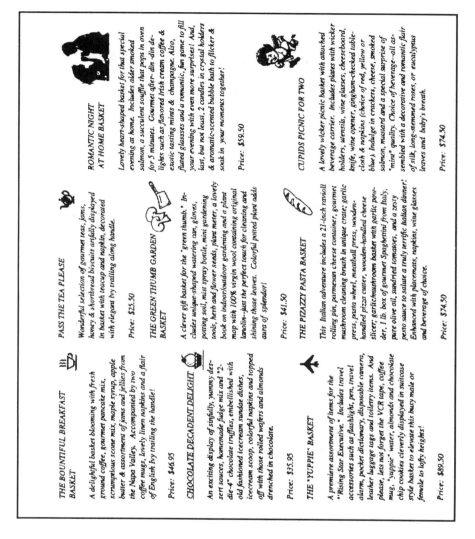

Inside Brochure

**THE BOUNTIFUL BREAKFAST BASKET**

A delightful basket blooming with fresh ground coffee, gourmet pancake mix, scrumptious scone mix, maple syrup, apple butter & assortment of jams and jellies from the Napa Valley. Accompanied by two coffee mugs, lovely linen napkins and a flair of English Ivy trailing the handle!

Price: $46.95

**CHOCOLATE DECADENT DELIGHT**

An exciting display of sinfully, yummy dessert sauces, homemade fudge mix and "2-die-4" chocolate truffles, embellished with old fashioned Icecream sundae dishes, icecream scoop, colorful napkins and topped off with those rolled wafers and almonds drenched in chocolate.

Price: $35.95

**THE "YUPPIE" BASKET**

A premiere assortment of items for the "Rising Star Executive." Includes travel accessories such as flashlight, pen, travel alarm, pocket dictionary, disposable camera, leather luggage tags and toiletry items. And please, lets not forget the VCR tape, coffee mug, "yuppie" water, almonds and chocolate chip cookies cleverly displayed in suitcase style basket to elevate this busy male or female to lofty heights!

Price: $89.50

**PASS THE TEA PLEASE**

Wonderful selection of gourmet teas, jams, honey & shortbread biscuits artfully displayed in basket with teacup and napkin, decorated with elegant Ivy trailing along handle.

Price: $25.50

**THE GREEN THUMB GARDEN BASKET**

A clever gift basket for the "green thumb." Includes unique-shaped watering can, gloves, potting soil, mist spray bottle, mini gardening tools, herb and flower seeds, plant meter, a lovely book on indoor/outdoor gardening and a plant mop with 100% virgin wool containing original lanolin—just the perfect touch for cleaning and shining those leaves. Colorful potted plant adds aura of splendor!

Price: $41.50

**THE PIZAZZY PASTA BASKET**

This Italian adventure includes a 21-inch ravioli rolling pin, parmesan cheese container, gourmet mushroom cleaning brush in unique crate; garlic press, pasta wheel, meatball press, wooden-handled pizza cutter, wooden-handled cheese slicer; garlic/mushroom basket with garlic powder, 1 lb. box of gourmet Spaghettini from Italy, pure olive oil, sundried tomatoes, and a zesty pesto sauce to salute a truly terrific Italian dinner! Enhanced with placemats, napkins, wine glasses and beverage of choice.

Price: $74.50

**ROMANTIC NIGHT AT HOME BASKET**

Lovely heart-shaped basket for that special evening at home. Includes alder smoked salmon, a succulent souffle that pops in oven for 5 minutes. Gourmet after-din-din delights such as flavored Irish cream coffee & exotic tasting mints & champagne. Also, fluted glasses and a romantic, fun game to fill your evening with even more surprises! And, last, but not least, 2 candles in crystal holders & aromatic-scented bubble bath to flicker & soak in your moments together!

Price: $59.50

**CUPIDS PICNIC FOR TWO**

A lovely wicker picnic basket with attached beverage carrier. Includes plates with wicker holders, utensils, wine glasses, cheeseboard, knife, wine opener, gingham-checked tablecloth & napkins (choice of red, yellow or blue). Indulge in crackers, cheese, smoked salmon, mustard and a special surprise of "mint" quality. Choice of beverage—all assembled with a decorative and romantic flair of silk, long-stemmed roses, or eucalyptus leaves and baby's breath.

Price: $74.50

6. The inside third panel (left side) can be used for detailed information on how and where to purchase your gift baskets. Also this panel can be used to list details such as holiday gift basket themes, special terms and volume purchases for the holidays, testimonials from happy customers and a company profile.

7. Brochures designed to be self-mailers will have one panel (usually the outside middle, or backside) for the address label and postage. Include your company name, address, telephone number and company logo with a catchy message that will move the reader to open it immediately.

8. To achieve high impact design, readability and pleasing appearance, remember to bring contrast to the design of your brochure by using white space. Don't cram too much text — give it breathing room. For example, surround a photo with a white border; use ragged, right column alignment; or increase space between text.

9. Maintain consistency. Have panels flow by keeping the margins, typeface and style, line spacing, headlines, subheads and captions uniform.

10. If using illustrations for basket themes, never let your product description bury your basket design. Stone, in *Successful Direct Marketing Methods*, says "The copy should never detract from the graphic presentation but should be used subliminally to inform and enhance."

11. Remember that the design of your brochure should enable the reader to follow from upper left to lower right.

12. Creatively name your basket categories with minimal wording such as Get Well, Baby, Birthday, Chocolate Lover, etc.

13. When writing about the items you carry, eliminate too much verbiage, but use descriptive phrasing. This script can also be memorized and used in your telephone sales presentations. Use unique phraseology that will catch the customer's attention, i.e., the Sports Basket — "An ideal and practical gift for the sports buff who has everything." Then highlight the products in the basket. Use words such as embellished with instead of filled with; whimsical instead of fun; extravagant instead of big; elegant or charming instead of beautiful; delightful, hilarious, enchanting, carefree, instead of cheerful, and so on.

14. Where you need captions for your written material, try to be clever. Use catchy phrases such as A Unique Gift Service for Discriminating People; Flexibility Is Our Forte; Baskets Blooming with Goodies; Gifts that Make the Magic Last!

15. Pick quality paper when choosing the stock. Talk to your printer about paper stock, prices, quantity and adding color. Prices vary appreciably when adding color. Sometimes it is worth the extra money to create an outstanding brochure. Using a professional graphic designer would definitely enhance your brochure if this fits into your budget.

**Sample Brochure Folds**

**8½" × 11" ONE FOLD**

**8½" × 3¹¹/₁₆" TWO FOLD**

## Fliers

Fliers are an excellent and relatively cost effective way of advertising your business especially during the holidays. Fliers make it possible for you to reach many shoppers. They can be distributed to local business merchants, doctor and dentist offices, banks, apartment complexes, and real estate offices by the thousands resulting in a great deal of business. In addition, you can use a specific holiday theme and design your flier around that theme to help people identify the value of associating your gift baskets with the holiday.

The example given here is one we used for the Christmas holiday season. By using red paper with black lettering, we designed a flier that was so unique and distinctive that frazzled holiday shoppers just had to stop and read it.

**STUMPED FOR A**
# HOLIDAY GIFT IDEA?

*OFFERING UNIQUE CUSTOM-DESIGNED GIFT BASKETS
AND DECOR FOR FAMILY, FRIENDS, CLIENTS, AND EMPLOYEES*

*THE FIRST CHRISTMAS OF THE '90s REPRESENTS A
NEW DECADE IN GIFT GIVING. SO, THIS YEAR "GIFT"
THEM WITH SOMETHING SPECIAL....A GIFT OF
QUALITY AND DISTINCTION THAT IS ALSO
FUNCTIONAL, DECORATIVE AND ......FOREVER!*

*FEATURING OUR EXCITING SPECIALTY FOOD BASKETS IN ALL PRICE RANGES*

*Those Bloomin' Baskets, etc.™*

*Because of the heavy Holiday demand,
Those Bloomin'Baskets, etc .tm
is requesting that you place your
order early so that we may
give the very best quality and
service possible.*

*Give the gift of distinction ...It is such a
wonderful and warm way to say
we care about you!*

*CALL (213) 379-7797 AND ASK FOR CAMILLE*

Holiday Flier

## Yellow Pages

Yellow Pages present a very sensible approach to advertising your Specialty Gift Basket Business. Because of the fact that the buying public has been conditioned over the years to "let their fingers do the walking" through the Yellow Pages, it makes sense to take advantage of that media. However, buying advertising in the Yellow Page has to be well planned as to the size of the advertisement and which Yellow Page Directory will give you the best return on your investment.

We have found that having a logo (a line drawing representative of your company) and the advertisement set in red type distinguished the ad from the others and made it easy for potential customers to find us. When you're ready to place your Yellow Page ad, it would be wise to research and see how other basket companies are positioned, the size, copy, and which directory is being used. Another suggestion is to make sure that the Yellow Page directory has a classification under "Gift Baskets."

## Newspaper Advertising

If you consider running ads in the newspaper, we recommend that you select community or local newspapers as opposed to the major metropolitan newspapers. The primary reason is that many times with local or community papers you will get more ad value for your dollar. Also for advertising to work effectively, it must be repetitive. However, if you have a large budget for advertising in newspapers and can sustain a consistency of repeated ads week after week, there is no question that major newspaper advertising will bring greater results, particularly during peak holiday seasons.

## Post Cards and Letters

Post cards and letters are excellent to use as a reminder or follow-up to your brochure and as a stand alone promotional piece for marketing your services to meeting and convention planners, promoters, associations, political action committees, clubs, organizations and corporations.

Letters work especially well for introducing your services to these markets. Post cards are effective during the holiday season. If a potential company or client hasn't responded to your brochure and there are only seven to ten days until Christmas, simply send them a card stating "I sincerely hope you have completed your Christmas shopping. However, if you haven't and time is running out then why not let us ease your stress with gifts of quality and distinction. Give a one-of-a-kind Specialty Gift Basket. We deliver! Happy Holiday Season."

## Thank You and Holiday Cards

Thank you cards and holiday cards serve several purposes and are effective tools in an ongoing advertising campaign. Cards can be designed to say "Thank you for your business." This keeps customers thinking of you and makes the customer feel appreciated.

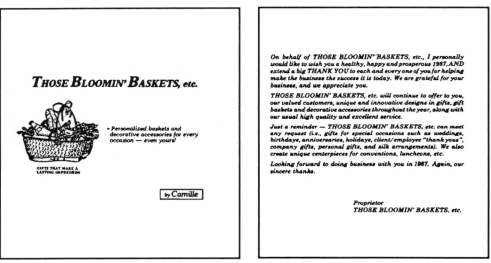

*Front and Inside of Card (Phone and address on the back)*

Cards can be designed and used to preview a holiday "Early Bird" special. You can be innovative in your direct mail advertising and promotion. Using post cards is an inexpensive and efficient way of keeping your old customers coming back year after year. Send out a Mother's Day post card suggesting a beautiful and elegant basket for that special lady. It is worth the time and record keeping to send out Birthday, Anniversary, Get Well, Christmas, and Hanukkah notes. Keep the idea of your gift baskets in the mind of your customers.

## *Your Car as a Promotion Vehicle*

Have magnetic signs with the name of your business, logo and telephone number made to put on the side of your car. This will cost less than $150 and is a legitimate business deduction. It is a terrific way to get your name around town. People do look and observe. Create a sign that will grab their attention.

*I use personalized license plates reading "BSKT LDY." This was a real conversation starter. Wherever I went in the car, my gift basket business was in the eyes of the beholder.*

**Chapter 13**

# $P$ORTFOLIOS AND PHOTOGRAPHY

*"A picture is worth a thousand words."*

$P$ictures sell food, cars, you name it, and they sell your baskets if they are the right ones. So be sure to keep this old adage in mind when you compile your portfolio. It is important to have a professional portfolio assembled with photographs creatively arranged in a classy album, preferably in a rich, corporate color — nothing cutesy. Purchase the photographer-type albums available through local photography stores. Or a good quality standard photo album can be made to look very professional by customizing the cover. Use fabric or other types of decorative coverings as long as the affect remains professional. Give ample time and attention to the design and layout of your portfolio as this is your main selling tool. The following are a few tips to give you a helping hand.

First design a title page.

Unique, Specialty Gift Baskets
Exclusively Designed and Created by

*THOSE BLOOMIN' BASKETS, ETC.*

**"GIFT BASKETS THAT MAKE
A LASTING IMPRESSION!"**

Then add a statement about your business:

> *"Those Bloomin' Baskets, etc. has been in operation since 1981. It started with a single concept of providing picnic baskets that were both functional and decorative, and expanded into a line of gift baskets offering a diversity of themes along with custom-design. We take pride in our work and the authenticity of our gift basket creations. We have had tremendous response to our executive and personalized gift-giving service.* Those Bloomin' Baskets, etc. *has something to offer — gift baskets that are distinctive, decorative, yet keenly discriminating, and they appeal to males and females of all ages!"*

Photographic displays should be neatly mounted. Include different themes and show five to seven baskets in low, medium, and high price ranges. Photographs displayed in the best portfolios are often enlarged and neatly mounted on heavy stock paper with protective sheets.

Include a brief description of each basket strategically placed underneath the photo with the theme name of the basket and a brief paragraph describing the contents of the basket. Use colorful wording such as — Just say Ole! Perfect South of the Border gourmet palate pleasers including natural tortilla chips, spicy salsa, mouth-watering chili and seasonings tucked in with a ceramic chip and dip duo, and of course, your favorite beverage to cool those taste buds!

If you list prices in your portfolio, place the price below each photo or use categories for price ranges. For example: Category "A" can include all baskets in the $12.95 to $25.95 price range; Category "B" from $26.00 to $44.95; Category "C" from $45.00 to $65.95; and Category "D" over $65.00.

Include in your statement about your business how your clients can benefit (receiving unique gifts, quality, convenience, promote their company's image, employee loyalty, etc). Also mention the services you offer such as delivery terms, shipping, and special handling.

Add testimonials from other clients and photocopies of articles written about your business, if you have them. Protective covers are suggested. List any memberships in professional organizations. Remember, it is up to you to sell yourself so do not be modest.

Add a note or disclaimer when substituting baskets to protect yourself if you cannot order the exact size.

Example:

**TERMS AND CONDITIONS OF SALE**
DUE TO THE AUTHENTICITY AND UNIQUENESS OF
PRODUCT, BASKETS AND CONTENTS ARE SUBJECT TO
AVAILABILITY. SUBSTITUTION, IF NECESSARY, WILL BE OF
EQUAL VALUE (ON APPROVAL OF BUYER IF BUYER RE-
QUESTS).

Use a closing phrase like:
*"Those Bloomin' Baskets, etc." offers you concepts in gift baskets
and decor that are avant-garde. they are:*
UNIQUE
DISTINCTIVE
DRAMATIC
ELEGANT — YET
KEENLY DISCRIMINATING

*THESE GIFT BASKETS WILL MAKE A LASTING IMPRESSION
ON THOSE SPECIAL CLIENTS. DO NOT FORGET TO GIFT
THEM ON SPECIAL OCCASIONS. ALSO — IMPRESS THOSE
SPECIAL PEOPLE IN YOUR LIFE BY GETTING YOUR NAME
INTO OUR EXECUTIVE CLIENT FILE. WE WILL REMEMBER
ALL OF THOSE SPECIAL PEOPLE AND DATES IN YOUR LIFE
BY DELIVERING TO THEM A VERY UNIQUE GIFT BASKET!*

# Photographing Your Baskets

**P**lan ahead and have your basket designs assembled for each
season and then you can photograph your baskets for your
portfolio. Because gift baskets are very attractive, capitalize on
their photogenic qualities. Carefully select the baskets that you wish
to display in your portfolio with an eye toward visual appeal and
color coordination.

You might decide to photograph your baskets outside, taking
advantage of a natural setting and the natural light. The best time for
an outdoor setting is during a slightly overcast day without bright

sun and shadows. Remember that your basket is the focal point, and the setting should complement the look and appeal of the basket.

If you photograph your baskets inside, choose a backdrop that will make the basket stand out. If you have a light-colored carpet, this might be just the right background.

*After experimenting with many different backdrops and settings, I found that background paper purchased from a photography supply or art store, works the best. One year, I photographed all of my holiday baskets with a light green background paper which made it quite festive with the reds and greens, golds and silvers in the baskets.*

Camille J. Anderson

For a year-round, professional looking background, a light grey is excellent. Ask in the photography supply store what they think would be the best. Experiment with different colors. Look in magazines and decorator books to get an idea of what colors might be appropriate.

Correct inside lighting is an important aspect of photography. If you are a novice, allow enough takes for experimentation. A few shots with a Polaroid camera would be helpful in attaining the best possible shot.

You can also use props in your photographs as long as they do not take away from the quality and contents of the baskets. Use props tastefully and remember that less is more. Be consistent. If you have holly boughs and pine cones in one shot, then those props should appear in all the others.

If photography is not your forte, or you simply don't want to put the energy into it and you want super quality photos, pay a friend who enjoys this type of work or pay a college student. Contact a community, city or state college or university. The students would love to get the experience and would be thrilled to be paid. If your budget allows, have a professional photographer take pictures of your baskets.

Keep in mind that you want your photographs to look as professional as possible — they represent your work.

**Chapter 14**

# SELLING STYLES AND TECHNIQUES

*"It is unwise to do unto others as you would have them do unto you. Their tastes may not be the same."*

— George Bernard Shaw

Clearly identifying the different roles you'll play in managing the business is one of the more important aspects of your gift basket business. Recognize that sales, marketing and customer service are three separate technologies. When integrated, they promote greater sales success and customer satisfaction.

There are different sales strategies and selling approaches for the various market segments that you'll be servicing. Calling on and obtaining a corporate client will sometimes require many repeat calls before you receive your first order, whereas calling on a small real estate office or insurance firm may illicit an immediate impulse purchase.

Here is a breakdown of four basic sales styles to match market environments and help you identify the different kinds of selling styles best suited to your personality.

1. THE CLOSER — A salesperson who, in most cases, makes the one-time, or at most two-time contact with a prospect. This salesperson works the numbers — the more prospects called on, the more single sales multiply. This sales approach requires that the salesperson quickly establish a rapport with the prospect and create an emotional desire and need for the product.

* Characteristics of the *Closer* — high energy and competitiveness. They are extroverted and driven, have strong egos, and are highly self-confident. They are theatrical in behavior and are able to create a sense of urgency and enthusiasm.

2. THE CONSULTANT — The *Consultant* usually goes for the high volume, high-ticket items. This salesperson is both patient and excellent with interpersonal skills along with being aggressive. Multiple sales calls to a potential client who needs special consultation and customized service is the forte of the *consultant.*

* Characteristics of the *Consultant* — self-confident, patient, status and image conscious, team-oriented, organized, technically competent and quick to develop interpersonal relationships with potential prospects.

3. THE RELATIONSHIP BUILDER — These salespeople generally build relationships over a very long period of time. Sales are dependent on the relationship of the salesperson and the prospect, and will generate some business eventually.

* Characteristics of the *Relationship Builder* — patient, persistent, dependable, knowledgeable about product, and are task- and time-management oriented.

4. DISPLAY — The display salesperson is your department store retail clerk, or one who sells from a booth at a fair, craft show, or flea market. The sale is primarily dependent on the product selling itself and this requires little personal involvement on the part of the salesperson.

* Characteristics of the Display Salesperson — Service-oriented, congenial, knowledgeable about product and averse to high pressure.

Regardless of which selling style you most predominantly employ in your Specialty Gift Basket Business, you'll find that the art of conversation and asking questions, coupled with good listening skills, create a powerful form of persuasion in what we call conversational selling.

Conversational selling is based on being able to ask the right questions to convince the customer to buy. Most people associate a salesperson personality with the idea that they talk a person into doing or buying something. However, research reveals that good selling requires a combination of verbal and nonverbal questions whereby we create the ALL-PRO system of selling. All-Pro is an acronym for Ask, Listen, Learn, Present, Respond, and Originate. This represents the verbal techniques as well as incorporating the nonverbal persuasion strategies.

An illustration of a nonverbal question would be a slight tilting of the head, leaning forward, or raising an eyebrow — all signify that you are listening and encourages the other person to give you more information.

Ask questions to solicit information about potential customer needs, interests, wants, and the budget they have allocated. Every customer has an intent or "hidden agenda" when they order. If you know the specific reason a customer is thinking about ordering, you will learn how to expose their hidden agenda by asking questions.

*"Successful salespeople never quit asking."*

— Don L. Price

## Questions to Ask Clients in Conversational Selling

Many customers have definite ideas about what they want, but most are open to suggestions. The best way to approach a potential customer when they place an inquiry, either by telephone or in person, is to ask the following questions:

1. Is the gift for a male or female?

2. What is your price range?

3. Is there a special occasion, i.e., a birthday, anniversary, baby gift or thank you? Do you have a certain theme in mind, i.e., sports, occupational or regional theme?

4. What foods are preferred by the recipient? Are they vegetarians, gourmet eaters, chocolate lovers? Do they enjoy certain types of food such as Italian, Mexican, Asian, Cajun, etc?

5. What colors do you want? What are the recipient's favorite colors? (If you can, find out the decor of their home and then you can personalize even more.)

6. Many times you can determine color by the theme. For example, when creating a basket with a Mexican theme, you can use

bright colors such as orange, blue, yellow, and green — repeat the colors in the place mats and napkins to tie it all together.

7. If the customer doesn't really have definite ideas in mind, suggest that you will create something very special with a variety or mix using your specialty products—then name a few.

8. If the customer wants a mid-range priced basket ($25-$50), suggest a sure-fire winner using a combination of coffees, teas, chocolates, or unique desserts and preserves. Be sure to include napkins, cups, stuffed animals, or other unique gifts.

☞ LISTEN actively with enthusiasm to learn how the customers want to be sold. Find out what their true objectives are and how you can best serve their needs.

☞ LEARN by listening to your customers. Find out what they want, what their price range is, and their reasons for buying. Then you can overcome any buying objections that may come up.

☞ PRESENT your program based on what you have learned from your prospective customer.

☞ RESPOND to their questions as you make your presentation. Meet their objectives and build their confidence in you. In order to get their account, ask for the order and close the sale.

Here is an example of how to use conversational selling by utilizing the acronym ALL-PRO system.

---

CUSTOMER: "Your baskets are lovely. However, I'm not sure a basket would be the right gift for him."

SALESPERSON: "Many men enjoy receiving our specialty gift baskets. What is the special occasion?"

CUSTOMER: "It's a job promotion with a new company."

SALESPERSON: "Is this the special man in your life?"

CUSTOMER: "Yes he is. We're engaged to be married next year and I am so proud of him."

SALESPERSON: "Congratulations to both of you. I can understand why you want to get just the right gift for him. What types of gifts have you given him in the past?"

CUSTOMER: "He's a sports fan and a great tennis player, so it's usually something related to sports and his favorite drink."

SALESPERSON: "I have the perfect idea for you that he's absolutely going to love. You say he's an athlete — what other sports does he enjoy besides tennis?"

CUSTOMER: "Skiing and bicycling."

SALESPERSON: "We'll create the perfect 'Jock' specialty gift basket with his favorite beverage, special foods, new tennis balls and several items related to bicycling. It'll be perfect for him."

CUSTOMER: "Terrific what a great gift idea. What will it cost?"

SALESPERSON: "How much did you plan to spend?"

CUSTOMER: "I was thinking of about $65.00 to $75.00."

SALESPERSON: "That's fine. What are his favorite colors and what types of food does he like?"

CUSTOMER: "Blue and yellow are his favorite colors, and he loves peanuts, jerky and things like canned oysters."

SALESPERSON: "When did you want to give him his gift?"

CUSTOMER: "Tonight."

---

There will be times when a customer is not able to make a decision as quickly as we have just demonstrated, especially if you are calling on major corporations and other business accounts. There is a selling strategy commonly referred to as the *leave behind* or *puppy dog sale*. The term puppy dog sale comes from the idea that when a person has had the "puppy dog" (your gift basket) around to look at, play with, cuddle and fall in love with, they take on the ownership and resist any idea of returning the "puppy dog." This strategy can have a positive effect on increasing your business as well as giving add-on sales and up-scaling your sales.

Here is how it works. Let's say you encounter a customer who is having a difficult time making a decision on the price and size of a gift they would like to give their clients for Christmas. Tell your customer that you will assemble a sample of three sizes of specialty gift baskets in the price range the client is considering and you will deliver them to the office. Tell your customer that you will be back in two days to pick up your sample specialty gift baskets and to take an order. When you prepare your samples, use a theme that meets the needs of your customer. Prepare a budget basket, a medium-priced one and a high-end, expensive one all in the same theme. After careful consideration the customer will almost always buy the high-end basket. The important thing to remember is that you will use various selling techniques and styles in your Specialty Gift Basket Business. Here are a few key pointers to keep uppermost in your mind.

☞ First impressions sometimes make or break a sale. Be a person you yourself would like to buy from, using all your wit and charm and showing interest in the client.

☞ Dress professionally and to fit the occasion.

☞ Know your sales presentation backwards and forwards and show excitement and enthusiasm toward your product and business.

☞ Have an attitude of flexibility and be willing to design a gift basket for almost any occasion with a price that is affordable.

☞ Always emphasize the concept of "PERSONALIZED BASKETS"— they are special and no one else will receive the same gift. *A one-of-a-kind gift for a one-of-a-kind person.*

☞ Be creative and have the ability to respond quickly to your clients' feelings and needs. In selling "personalized gift baskets" there are two objectives: create the relationship and close the sale.

Someone once said that nothing happens until someone sells something. In your Specialty Gift Basket Business you have to make it happen. You have to sell, and how you sell is dependent on your specific marketing plan. However, there are eight steps critical to your selling success.

The first three are generally associated with marketing.

*Company Image Building*
*Client Lead Generation*
*Client Qualifying*

The second three are related to the sales process.

*Presentation*
*Answering Objections*
*Closing the Sale*

The last two are service directed:

*Customer Relations*
*Customer Service*

1. **Company Image Building**: Image is built over a period of time with many factors contributing, such as quality products, excellent service, fair market pricing, trust, credibility and reliability.

2. **Client Lead Generation:** Obtain through high impact name recognition using marketing techniques such as direct mail, Yellow Pages, seminars, press releases, editorial recognition in your community, print advertising, radio advertising, and direct canvassing. The most cost effective will be a continuous chain of referrals from your satisfied customers.

3. **Client Qualifying:** Identify prospects as "not interested," "interested," "not ready," "ready." Some prospects may be interested but not ready — their event or party may be three months away. Others might not be interested now, not ready now, but perhaps will be interested five months from now. Then there are prospects who are ready now.

4. **Presentation:** Always be prepared with a professional presentation about your products and service that can be given in one minute to one hour in length. You never know when you will need a snappy yet professional one-minute presentation for those chance encounters — when you are waiting for the elevator. Use a more detailed sales pitch when you have the time. The one-hour could be a seminar to a group of real estate agents selling them on the idea of giving gift baskets to their clients.

5. **Client Objection:** An inexperienced salesperson can be overwhelmed by the number of questions a prospective customer asks. Do not feel defeated — you have not lost the battle. Often the client is just looking for a logical reason to buy a gift basket — so be sure to give one. For example, the cost is right, it is a practical gift that will be used rather than set aside, it saves the client time, and you will deliver the basket promptly.

6. **Closing the Sale**: Closing is simply ASKING for and getting the order. You will improve your closing ratios as you improve your selling skills.

Zig Ziglar said, "good closing comes from good selling and good people." A study conducted by the New York Sales and Marketing Club, indicated 71% of the people who buy from you do so because they like you, trust you, and respect you.

Asking for the order can be as simple as looking directly into the eyes of your customer, speaking firmly and deliberately, and ending with a closing statement or question such as: "This is a special gift going to a special person. Let's go ahead and select the right colors and that perfect wine."

7. **Customer relations:** Position you, your baskets, and your business firmly in the mind of your past, existing, and future clients. Positioning is critical when your product can be used on a regular basis. Companies large and small have different hierarchies — from upper level management to line level employees and from one department to one hundred — all of which are likely prospects for your Specialty Gift Basket Business.

8. **Customer Service:** Top quality products and excellent service are essential for customer loyalty.

*"There is only one boss... the customer. And he can fire everybody in the company from the chairman on down, simply by spending his money somewhere else."*

— Sam Walton, Founder Wal-Mart

**Chapter 15**

# GOOD CUSTOMER RELATIONS AND CORPORATE ACCOUNTS

*"A little bit of quality*
*Will always make 'em smile;*
*A little bit of courtesy*
*Will bring 'em in a mile;*
*A little bit of friendliness*
*Will tickle 'em 'tis plain—*
*And a little bit of service*
*Will bring 'em back again."*
— Anonymous

Maintaining excellent customer relations is paramount in any business. The one thing that keeps you in business is responding to the demands of the marketplace and that marketplace is the people.

Unlike many businesses, the Specialty Gift Basket Business has very few, if any, problems with refunds and returns. However, if a customer complains about your product, take immediate steps to correct any problems. There is a saying we use in our training classes: "Good news travels fast... BAD news travels faster." Don't let your company be the bearer of bad news.

*Recently we shipped about 45 specialty arrangements to an eight year-old corporate account. In the shipping, one of the arrangements was damaged. When the customer informed us of the damage, we immediately shipped a replacement. The issue was not how the damage occurred, but only to satisfy the need of the customer.*

## Corporate Accounts

**M**arketing and selling to small, medium and large corporations can double or triple your sales in one year. In order to obtain these accounts and keep them, you must understand how to open doors and create your niche in the markeplace. Be an astute business person who is organized and prepared. It is imperative to have a marketing and selling strategy. The idea is to get so close to the corporation that when a holiday, birthday, anniversary, graduation, promotion or some other special event occurs, you are the first person they think of. Getting on the inside of the corporation is the key to your success. The way to create viable relationships in any company is to provide a quality product, quality service, and a sincere desire to be there to help people solve their gift-giving problems and save them time.

One of the factors you should emphasize is the relatively low cost. Big corporations often give expensive leather briefcases, boxes of wine, or other similar expensive gifts to their clients. You can step in and offer them a very elegant and showy gift that will actually save them money as well as give them a gift-giving solution, and you do all the work.

More and more companies are using incentive programs that include such perks as travel to faraway places, two tickets to a sporting event or dinner for two at a famous dinner house, flowers for a birthday, or a specialty gift basket for a promotion, or thank you gift.

Big businesses, corporations, and even smaller companies who want to make a lasting impression on their clients and who want the image of their firm to stand out, give gifts. They search for items that are distinctive enough to survive the wastebasket and to keep their company's name before their customers year-round. Gift baskets are the perfect solution and getting those corporate accounts is big business for you. In short, specialty gift baskets rank high in corporate gift-giving.

Additional business can be developed by creating centerpieces for meetings, special events, conventions, banquets, fund-raisers, ethnic events, and Secretary's Day, just to name a few.

What are large companies or corporations looking for?

- ☞ Convenience and service with an emphasis on saving time
- ☞ Dependability and quality in product and service
- ☞ Honesty and reliability
- ☞ Professional literature about the product
- ☞ Timing, call backs, and mailing updates
- ☞ Friendly rapport
- ☞ Personalization
- ☞ Working within their allotted budget

## Who Do You Contact?

Try to find out who is involved in buying gifts for employee functions or client meetings such as employee service awards, Christmas raffles, client gifting, etc. Many times within a corporation there are multiple groups, internal clubs such as Toastmasters, ski clubs, political action groups and various departments which you would contact separately. If the corporation is large enough, it may have a meeting planner, a special events coordinator, and a day-care center. Do your research or make contact with someone within the company to meet the right person.

## Approaching the Corporation

It is advisable to send the company your pre-approach sales letter along with your brochure first. Follow up no later than three days with a phone call and make an appointment. For mid-size to large corporations who see salespeople all day long, you will get better results by sending a packet of information to two or three people within the organization such as a secretary, a sales or personnel representative. Remember to address all mail-outs professionally by using proper titles. However, there is nothing wrong with "cold calling" on large companies. Many times just stopping in and talking to the front desk receptionist will help you gain access to the company's list of department heads and corporate officers. If you can obtain a corporation's annual report, you have a gold mine of information and people to contact.

The key to opening up and gaining access to other departments is through referrals. When talking with the personnel manager, ask to be personally introduced to other department heads. Get appointments with the personnel manager, marketing manager, sales manager, special events manager, secretaries, union shop steward, and if they have a day-care center, contact the administrator to make a sales presentation.

The following points will help you in your pursuit of success:

1. Give personal service.

2. Promotion — Mail fliers, brochures and sales material that will grab their attention.

*The way that we targeted corporate accounts was by creating a unique "mail-out." In this mail-out we included an actual color photo of a holiday basket to enhance the idea, show the quality and uniqueness of the baskets, and to appeal to the senses and emotions. The whole package exuded a "feeling of Christmas." It was visually pleasing and the display of specialty food items tantalized their taste buds. We also had a card printed in green ink emphasizing the gourmet foods that Those Bloomin' Baskets, etc. was featuring that particular holiday season. To add another homey touch, we tied a thin red ribbon with our enclosure tags and enclosed this in a handmade, cloth envelope with a festive, executive print. Everything was placed in 5 x 7 mailing envelopes.*

- Visual Presentation: Assemble a professional portfolio with quality photos. If you can have your baskets photographed professionally, do so, or at least, invest in a good 35 mm camera that takes close-ups. (See Chapter 13 on Portfolios and Photography.)

- After you send the brochure or letter, follow up with a phone call three days later and stress the benefits of your service.

- For office presentations or personal introductions, take a prepared gift basket with you and make sure it is impressive! If you are so inclined, develop a video to advertise your services and products to send to interested corporate accounts. As another approach, feature a collectible or unique basket or other item. By doing this, your sales emphasis can be that the recipient will have a lasting memory of the sender's thoughtfulness.

- Know your customers. Anticipate their needs. Individualize gift designs to the type of corporation such as, chocolate computer for computer firm; toy truck for construction company, tire for tire stores, plumbing gadget, etc.

- Corporate Gift Registry: Promote a year-round account by selling the idea of keeping track of personal days (wife's birthday, Secretary's Day, Valentine's Day, etc.). Get a list of who they send gifts to, and all other pertinent information. Tell them you will take care of all their special occasion gifts for the year. This will push your gift basket business to the pinnacle of success! Have forms ready for them to fill out and then start your "tickler file" for each account and flag your calendars. (A tickler file is a special file to remind one of specific dates for the future.)

3. Service the account. You must be prepared to meet the high demand and big profits by:

- Be prepared. Have the ability to design a large number of gift baskets within a specified time frame, tailoring your baskets in such a way that your business client is recognized as the giver. If necessary, line up part-time help for the basket assembly. This is a good time to get your family involved. Rent extra space for assembling and storage of baskets if your volume dictates.

- Be set up for last-minute additional orders. This is not unusual during the holidays. As Christmas and Mother's Day draw near, people panic. Be fully stocked with merchandise or know that your suppliers and wholesalers can deliver fast. Make sure you have plenty of supplies such as excelsior and decor. If you can handle this demand, it will add the stamp of approval to your name, and give you repeat business and referrals — and that means PROFITS!

One of the many rewards of adding that company to your client list by successfully filling the order, is that there will be many "happy returns." For example, the car dealership that ordered 60 holiday baskets can become your first reorder for the next season. Those who received one of the baskets, whether staff, personnel, or other clients, are next in line to order if they really liked what they got. Make sure your business card and an enclosure card with all pertinent information is in each basket.

4. Plan your deliveries down to the nth degree. (See Chapter 11, Making Deliveries.)

## Presentation Skills

Books written on the subject of presentation skills all share a common thread — people make up their minds within the first few minutes whether they like you or not. This is critical to selling, and simply means that you must be completely aware of how you come across to other people. In his book, *You are the Message,* Roger Ailes said, "If you could master one element of personal communications that is more powerful than anything we've discussed, it is the quality of being likeable." A survey done by the American Management Association of Business Executives asked what was the number one need for success in business today. Their response was: "To persuade others of your value and the value of your ideas."

The Specialty Gift Basket Business is a creative and rewarding business. However, for some people who have never called on corporate accounts it can seem somewhat intimidating. Therefore, learn good selling skills to help diminish the fears, build self-confidence, and channel your nervousness when conducting and making presentations.

*"There is perhaps nothing so bad and so dangerous in life as fear."*
— Jawaharlal Nehru

Most people can't resist a sincere bright smile and warmth beaming from the eyes. This says, "I like you and believe in myself and my product." However, belief in yourself and your baskets is not enough. Preparation is the major key to success in working with corporations. Prepare your materials and presentation well. Corporation executives expect you to be professional in every aspect. Their time is important so assure them that your presentation will be brief. Offer to bring "tasting samples" — they can see, smell and taste a sample of the good things that go into the basket.

Because you don't want to take up the corporate client's valuable time, first impressions are critical, and in all probability, you'll only have one chance to make a presentation to them. Listed below are key pointers to successfully maintain an ongoing relationship with corporate accounts.

\* Plan and stick by your objective. (Is it to make a presentation, generate a qualified lead, build your centers of influence, or deliver your order?)

\* Be Prepared — Know something about the company you will give the presentation to — their product, logo, size and what their budget might be. Incorporate what you know about them into a sample gift basket you will show them, along with fold-outs of alternatives in ribbons and designs.

Marketing comes before selling. Create your business image with professional looking stationery, business cards, note enclosures, and envelopes — all matching in color and texture and imprinted with your logo, current address and telephone numbers. Everything from your stationery to your brochures should be professionally typeset and printed. DO NOT USE DOT MATRIX. People, especially in corporations, associate professional marketing brochures and fliers with the quality of your product.

\* Picture yourself as your clients see you. Let them know that you are willing to work with them to meet their future gift-giving needs.

\* Be flexible. Know that when what you are doing doesn't work, you have the flexibility to change.

*"The graveyard of business is littered with companies that failed to recognize inevitable change."*

— Anonymous

\* When working with your corporate accounts always get a 50% deposit with the order, with the balance to be paid upon delivery. This will give you the cash flow to purchase additional or special inventory that you might not have in stock. This is an acceptable business practice.

\* Sign a typewritten contract stipulating the price, terms, conditions and delivery date.

---

**EXAMPLE OF CONTRACT LETTER**

## *THOSE BLOOMIN' BASKETS, etc.*

October 23, 1990

*Company*
*Address*

Dear Mr. Swift:

This letter is to confirm your order that we discussed on Saturday, October 22 for 30 Christmas gift baskets and decor at $35.00 each.

I will be providing a variety of unique custom-designed baskets consisting of my popular "duck in the vine basket" enriched with a blend of popular Christmas colors and embellished with the fresh touch of pine, holly, etc.

It was indeed a pleasure meeting with you. I know that Those Bloomin' Baskets will bring a smile to your client's faces and they will remember you every time they see the basket. What a way to impress them and let them know how you value their continued business with your company!

Please sign, date and return this contract letter with the requested deposit.

Best regards,

Camille J. Anderson
Those Bloomin' Baskets, etc.

Enc.

---

Every time you take an order, get a referral, or give a presentation, send out the appropriate THANK YOU card. It shows you have good manners and it is good business practice.

Always ask for testimonial letters from your clients. If the corporation has many divisions, ask for a personal introduction to the other divisions as well as a testimonial letter.

Know that you have a product that represents the best in gift giving and assume an attitude that everyone you meet needs your products and services.

CONTRACT FOR PROFESSIONAL SERVICES RENDERED

THIS AGREEMENT IS MADE BETWEEN THOSE BLOOMIN' BASKETS, etc. AND ███████████.

THOSE BLOOMIN' BASKETS, etc. WILL PROVIDE 30 DECORATIVE GIFT BASKETS AND CENTERPIECES AT $35.00 EACH FOR ██████ ██████ FOR A TOTAL OF $1026.42 (INCLUDES 10% DISCOUNT FOR VOLUME ORDER PLUS TAX AND DELIVERY CHARGE)

████████████ AGREES TO PAY A 50% DEPOSIT WHICH WOULD BE $513.21 ON OR BEFORE NOVEMBER 1, 1990 WITH THE BALANCE DUE ($513.21) ON THE DATE OF DELIVERY (DECEMBER 16, 1990).

| Breakdown of cost: | 30 baskets @ $35 = | $1050.00 | |
|---|---|---|---|
| | Minus 10% discount | -105.00 | |
| | | | $ 945.00 |
| | Plus sales tax (6.5%) | +61.42 | |
| | | | $ 1006.42 |
| | Plus delivery charge | 20.00 | |
| | Total | | $ 1026.42 |

| | | | |
|---|---|---|---|
| _____ | ____ | _____ | ____ |
| Those Bloomin' Baskets, etc. | Date | Signature for ██████████ | Date |

## How to Negotiate With Your Customers for Increased Sales

Webster defines negotiate as "to confer, bargain, or discuss with a view to reaching agreement." That statement implies that all relationships between people require negotiation to one degree or another.

Here is an example of ordinary day-to-day negotiations between a husband and wife. They arrive home at approximately the same time each evening. The husband suggests ordering a pizza for a quiet evening at home watching a video. The wife, not excited about pizza, suggests they go out for Chinese food. The process of resolving this difference without an argument is negotiation. Communication skills, flexibility and a sincere desire to please one's partner and at the same time fulfill personal needs is what negotiation is all about. Good negotiation means that both parties are satisfied.

The same rule applies in business, except business negotiations require planned strategies, being able to ask the right questions, good listening skills, and an ability to compromise and use diplomacy while getting action and results that are favorable to all parties involved.

To insure increased sales from your corporate clients, employ the following ideas in your negotiations.

➤ Listen to your clients when they talk — not only with your ears, but listen with your eyes as well. Your client may be saying one thing and picturing another.

To illustrate this point, let us assume that it is National Secretaries' Week, and your corporate client is giving specialty gift baskets to two executive secretaries. However, during your conversations the client mumbles to himself that he is concerned about how three other secretaries in the company will react. As you observe the concern reflected on his face, you suggest that you can help him solve this problem by adding three less expensive but equally satisfying gift baskets to give the other secretaries. Be ready to give him a volume discount on the extra three gift baskets. By making him feel that you have solved his problem, you have also expanded your order.

➤ Deal with people on their own terms as long as it represents both parties coming out the victors.

➤ Be willing to give up something in a negotiation that may be somewhat of lesser importance to you but very important to the other party. (In the illustration above, the corporate client was willing to solve his concern by paying a little extra, and you gave additional discount for volume.)

➤ Never put all your cards on the table. Leave yourself room to negotiate even after you have closed the sale.

➤ Knowledge of people and their behavior is essential to the negotiation process.

**Chapter 16**

# MOVING INTO A RETAIL STORE

*"Long-range planning does not deal with future decisions, but with the future of present decisions."*

—Peter F. Drucker

You have reached the point where you're about ready to burst right out of your home with baskets, baskets and more baskets. Your storage space has shrunk. You realize it is now time to consider moving into a retail store. What is the next step?

First of all, think of the many advantages there are to moving into a storefront operation:

✦ Greater accessibility and convenience for customers

✦ More room for displays and baskets

✦ The ability to create many gift baskets and store them with ease

✦ A more professional image

✦ Contacts with manufacturers and sales reps are more consistent and solid

✦ More repeat business

Your decision to open a retail store should be based on several factors — where you want to go with your business, marketing research, evaluation of client needs and desires, and all aspects of creative merchandising. Use an integrated market approach to encompass these factors.

✦ Research your marketplace, your competition and your image.

✦ Analyze and interpret all that information.

✦ After this data has been compiled, find a strategic location for your store. Choosing the right location can make or break a business.

Avenues for you to pursue in doing a marketing study are:

☐ Check into studies by your local chamber of commerce.

☐ Check into studies done by:

• Radio stations, newspapers and other media

• Department of Commerce

• Bureau of Consensus

• Surveys from consumer and trade magazines

• Surveys from government and business-oriented publications

☐ Get direct feedback from trade shows and seminars.

☐ Approach a college or graduate school marketing class to cost effectively implement a formal market research study.

☐ Call a local university and talk with the head of its marketing department. A student might like a class project, or a graduate student might want to take on this project for credit and a modest hourly fee. Also check your newspapers' classified section for ads placed by university and college students looking for start-up businesses that need marketing help. Students do the complete marketing study as a class project free of charge.

Once you have found a location for your retail store and are ready to set up shop, remember:

☐ Never take a commercial storefront lease for granted. Ask these specific questions before you sign a lease.

☐ How is my rent calculated? Rents are generally based on an annual cost per square foot. There are generally five variations for calculating rents.

- Gross lease — requires a flat monthly amount leaving the landlord responsible for all building expenses including taxes, insurance, and repairs.

- Net lease — requires a flat monthly amount and tenant paying some or all of the real estate taxes.

- Net-net lease — requires a flat monthly amount, and the tenant pays real estate taxes plus insurance on the occupied space.

- Net-net-net lease — referred to as a triple net lease. The tenant pays a flat monthly amount plus real estate taxes, insurance, repairs and maintenance.

- Percentage lease — applies to most retailers in multiple-tenant malls or shopping centers. The tenant pays a flat monthly amount plus a percentage of gross sales.

☐ How much and how will your rent go up?

- If you outgrow your retail space before your lease expires, can you sublease?

☐ Who pays for tenant improvements? Who legally owns the improvement when your lease expires?

☐ Do you have an option to renew your lease?

☐ Most importantly, you want to obtain legal advice before signing any lease.

Once the lease is signed — *voila* — here comes the creative-action-steps to take for being the most unique and unforgettable retail outlet in your community. There are many important factors to keep in mind.

## Store Design

✱ Be very selective in choosing wall coverings. Whether the wall is painted, textured or wallpapered, it should have durability and visual staying power.

✳ Lighting plays an important role in displaying your baskets. Research the best ways to use lighting to your advantage.

✳ Pedestals, wooden furniture, chairs, armoires, wicker, chest of drawers, benches, antique furniture, crates, cradles, ladders, wagons, etageres, hat and coat racks, to name a few, can help to create a great ambience. Or you can be more elegant with glass tables, glass-top tables and cubes to generate a more open atmosphere.

✳ Utilize every inch of space to your advantage.

✳ Use eye-catching displays to capture your customer's attention.

✳ Use blends and contrasting colors and patterns to attract attention. Vivid colors can be placed in an otherwise dark corner of the store with proper light. Remember, if properly displayed, an item will sell.

✳ Create vignettes in your store by using screens, dividers, etc.

# Creative Planning and Merchandising

✳ Make a statement in your store design and your products. Use signs but keep them brief, catchy and to the point. For example, you can use New Fall Decor, Terrific Buy, Latest Plaid Fashion, Christmas is Just Around the Corner.

✳ Motion attracts attention and you can draw customers to a particular display using wind chimes, balloons, streamers, etc.

✳ Offer other decorative accessories and items such as specialty gourmet food, stationery and cookware.

✳ Always have your ready-to-buy standard baskets on display in all price ranges.

✳ Change merchandising displays regularly.

## Sales Incentives for Your Customers

$ Strive to come up with new ideas for creative marketing and promotion. Hold open houses, in-house demonstrations and presentations for key holidays with complementary food and beverage samples you are featuring in your baskets.

$ Offer freshly brewed coffee and tea. It is a welcoming aroma, keeps customers in the store longer, and entices them to buy.

$ During the holidays, use the wonderful scents of the season by brewing various spices such as cinnamon, bayberry, cloves, etc.

$ Capitalize on your custom-designed baskets and personalized services.

$ Offer services such as an 800 number, wrapping, shipping and delivering.

$ Be flexible. Strive to deliver the same day. Remember these phrases, "we can", "we do," and "yes, we will."

$ Dress up for special occasions and deliveries (see Chapter 11).

## Sales and Marketing Ideas for Your Retail Store

Be aware of customers' needs, desires, interests, and changing values. Have in-store questionnaires available to get customer feedback. Talk to your customers and get their suggestions. Have a long-range advertising plan for your retail store. First, place an ad in the Yellow Pages of the telephone book. Use direct mail advertising such as, post cards, brochures, fliers and special holiday announcements. Newspaper ads, newspaper inserts and radio are also effective techniques to bring in those customers. Build your customer list from:

$ Sales and guest book

$ Lists from country clubs

$ Chamber of Commerce

$ Local sales and marketing clubs

$ Local women's groups and clubs

$ Real estate boards

$ Businesses and corporations

$ Zip code directories

# As a Retailer and Owner...

**D**o not compromise quality. Train your employees in the art of gift basket designing. Any time you hire employees, have thorough sales and customer service training programs. Develop a written personnel manual for your employees with specific information about company policy, sick pay, holidays, vacations, employee conduct, raise and salary reviews, their authority and responsibilities.

It is mandatory to find a good store manager or promote someone already on your staff as your assistant manager for times when you won't be there. You need someone who is trustworthy, conscientious, good with customers, and who has good selling skills. Last but not least, you need someone capable of helping you with basket design and store display.

Continue to keep your merchandise current by shopping through:

➤ Gift, basket and other trade shows

➤ Direct mail catalogs

➤ Sales representative's catalog sheets and brochures

➤ Trade advertisements in newspapers and magazines

➤ Wholesalers' catalogs

# Chapter 17

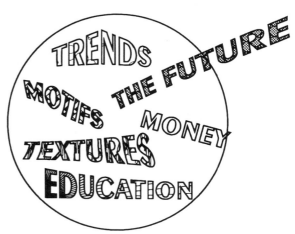

# KEEPING CURRENT IN THE INDUSTRY

*"Business more than any other occupation, is a continual dealing with the future: it is a continual calculation, an instinctive exercise in foresight."*
—Henry R. Luce

It is important to pay attention to color and design trends in apparel, home furnishings and interior decor as they eventually make their way into gifts, accessories and gift baskets and keep you state-of-the-art in your basket creations.

For example, wicker provides the consumer with a stylish accent at an affordable price. The market for wicker is changing. It is no longer just a whimsical accent for bath or bedroom. It has a more upscale look than it used to, and it is taking hold as a serious, high-style decorative accessory. Wicker now comes in a wide spectrum of colors other than just naturals and earth tones. It plays an important role in European Country design, especially in garden decor. White willow baskets are always popular. South Sea Island baskets, ranging from exotic to the very primitive, offer a uniqueness in patterns and weaves.

Designer baskets are available in painted motifs, some with stencil designs, others handpainted. Porcelain flowers are being used by some basket designers to garnish their baskets with something very special.

As mentioned in earlier chapters, floral design is a plus for the overall design of your basket. It will catapult you head over shoulders in front of your competition. Your customers will be more

attracted to the basket with floral design. The baskets look bigger, and this interprets to "more", and therefore, a higher sales price (sometimes 20 to 25 percent more). An added benefit for your customer is that they can use a basket with a good floral design as a centerpiece or an attractive decor item in their office.

Florals are just one aspect of basket enhancement. There are numerous ways to make the baskets "shine." Take a class in floral design or check out a book from the library in this area. It will not only increase your profits, but it will give you an eye for design — shape, height, color and size. A well-designed basket is artistically created, never just products thrown together in a basket.

Today the accessory market is reflecting the consumer's interest and concern with animal protection. Artificial animals of every size, from domestic to exotic are being sold to consumers. Therefore, as basket designers, we should be aware of trends like this and create baskets with animal themes such as wild animals in a dramatic jungle motif.

## Environmental Issues

Large segments of the population are making buying decisions based on whether a product is good for the environment. This strong and growing niche called green marketing has its own special skills and presentation strategies and most definitely presents an opportunity for the basket designer and retailer to sell environmentally-conscious products, i.e., ecologically sound products, recycled greeting cards, journals, calendars, note cards, etc.

Have an environmental theme product — an environmental gift basket called Earth Basket in your line. The Earth Basket can consist of recycled greeting or note cards or stationery; flower seeds, a 100% homespun shopping bag, cedar sachet, unbleached coffee filters, and a terra cotta bird feeder. You can embellish the basket with dried grasses and florals or a live plant or flower that can be replanted.

It is a good idea to look into different biodegradable packaging ideas. Environmental awareness offers new profit opportunities and new ways to strengthen your image and long-term business goals.

## Keep on Learning

**E**arlier, in Chapter 9, we gave you some basic ideas on folding napkins. Buy or check out a napkin-folding book from your local library to further increase your skills in this area. You will use cloth napkins in a large percentage of your baskets — the more creative you can be in displaying them, the more pizazz it adds to your baskets.

Improve your knowledge and skills through seminars, symposiums, conventions, night classes, exchange forums and videos on subjects that can help you in this gift basket industry. Subjects could be in floral design, basket design, sales and marketing, profit-building ideas, or new equipment. Budget a certain amount of money and time each month for continuing education. Remember, LEARNING EQUALS PROFITS.

*" The return from learning can concern more earning"*
— Anonymous

## Trade Shows

**A**ttend gift products and accessory shows, gourmet food, craft and gift basket shows in your area. Trade shows are sources for purchasing new merchandise and also provide a wealth of display ideas. In addition, you get your name on catalog mailing lists and have the benefit of their representatives coming to you. The following tips are for browsing trade shows:

✦ Dress to be comfortable, but not sloppy.

✦ Wear comfortable shoes. You will cover a lot of territory.

✦ Set a budget and stick to it. Comparison shop for the best products, best prices, best packaging and best terms.

✦ Take advantage of educational seminars if you can.

✦ Bring plenty of business cards, and/or your gift basket tags (less expensive to pass out) with name, address and phone number. It is difficult to obtain a catalog without a business card.

✦ Bring a tote bag to carry catalogs and business cards, stapler, small calculator and credit information for filling out credit applications with vendors you would like to do business with in the future. Also include some information about your business as well as the ownership.

On your first few orders with various companies, you will no doubt have to pay C.O.D. until you build up your business credit. But don't lose faith, it will happen and then you are set!

Subscribe to newsletters, magazines on gift baskets, gifts, sales and marketing, etc., that will enable you to keep up on current trends in the gift and gourmet food industries. Here are six industry oriented magazines:

- Gifts & Decorative Accessories (212) 532-0651

- The Gourmet Retailer (800) 327-3736

- GR Gift Reporter (212) 532-0652

- Gift Basket Review (904) 634-1902

- Gift & Stationery Business (212) 869-1300

- Giftware News (609) 227-0798

For all who have read this book and who open up their gift basket business, we personally wish for you the very best of success. For the hobbyist or the reader who wanted additional ideas and information to assist in an existing business, we wish for your continued success.

We would like to finish with this thought:

*"One person sees a mountain as a mountain. Another takes it personally, as a thing to be climbed, or else. Awful as the climbing might be, the or-else is worse."*

Amy Gross, Writer

# Appendix A

# *T*AX DEUCTIONS

Tax laws change frequently. The Tax Reform Act of 1986 placed many new restrictions on the home/business issue. This Appendix contains information to be read with the awareness that we are in no way rendering legal, accounting, or other professional services. The intent is to provide tax information for home-based businesses. Detailed information, along with legal advice, will have to be obtained from your accountant, attorney, or the Internal Revenue Service (IRS).

## Tax Tips

☛ Keep clear, complete records of your income, expenses, assets (such as computer or typewriter) and liabilities (such as loans or notes) to help minimize your taxes and to defend yourself in the event you are audited. You must be able to substantiate any claim you make.

☛ Use a business credit card to obtain documentation for travel, entertainment and gas and oil purchases. Receipts back up your claims for business expenses.

☛ If you make a long-distance business call from a pay phone, which gives no receipt, create your own by writing down the expense and its business purpose on a piece of paper, in a log book or on an appointment calendar.

☛ Keep all records in safe place.

☛ The IRS has two basic criteria your home/office must meet in order to qualify as a tax write-off: "The portion of your home you wish to claim as a business expense must be used exclusively and regularly for business."

**Exclusive Use** means that the portion of your home you are claiming as a deduction is used only for business. Your home/office may be an entire room you have given over to that purpose or it may simply be a breakfast nook off your kitchen (one that is not used for dining). It must be a separately identifiable space. Think of your home/office (business space/work space) as a separate entity from your home.

**Regular Use** is when you use the business segment of your home on a continuing basis. You need to prove that you are using your business space regularly for so many hours of each day or week. Also, "the portion of your home you use exclusively and regularly for business must be either your principal place of business or a place where you meet with customers or clients in the normal course of business."

☛ Indirect expenses related to the entire home (mortgage payments, insurance, utility bills, roof repair), are deductible IN PART. One way to arrive at a percentage figure is to divide the square footage of your "work space" by the total square footage of your home. You can also calculate the deductible portion of your home by dividing the number of rooms used for business by the total number of rooms in your home.

☛ If you have a single telephone line into the home, you will not be able to deduct telephone charges to your business. Once your business is established, install a separate business line so that you can claim the allowable business deduction. If you run an ad in the Yellow Pages, the monthly charge is deductible.

☛ You can deduct meal expenses up to 80 percent when taking a customer out and only if it is directly related to the active conduct of a taxpayer's business. However, you always need to substantiate this with meticulous records in your daily log or diary. You need to note on the receipt who you entertained, where, why, and how much. The IRS will disallow any expense that you cannot substantiate.

☛ Business gifts are deductible at the current limit of up to $25 per business associate. Always give your customer a receipt showing who bought the basket and to whom it was delivered — the customer needs the information for tax purposes. A large percentage of our customers are businesses such as realty companies who are gifting others to say *"thank you."*

☛ Whenever you leave home to meet with business contacts, do work-related research at the library, buy office supplies or postage, purchase inventory, negotiate a contract, or attend a work-related class or meeting, you are making a business trip. It is very important that you keep a log of your business and non-business travel if you also use your car for trips that are just personal.

☛ If you use public transportation, such as buses, subways, or taxis (get a receipt from taxi driver), record the date, destination, cost, and purpose of each trip in a travel diary. If you mainly travel in your own vehicle, log all business-related mileage. The alternative is to calculate what percentage of your overall car use is devoted to business and take that percentage of your total automobile expenses (including gasoline, repairs, maintenance, insurance and depreciation) as your deduction.

☛ Take photos of office/work space, gift basket display, inventory storage, delivery vehicle with baskets, etc. They can only enhance records.

☛ Deduct business club dues and lunches when in the ordinary and necessary course of your business.

☛ Deduct home entertainment — getting referrals, entertaining prospects. Record in a diary. Save grocery receipts. If you hold an "Open House" for the showing of your baskets, take photos and save receipts for food, beverage and other items.

On the following page is a list of suggested business expenses related to the gift basket business and eligible for deduction.

- ☐ Accounting
- ☐ Advertising and promotion
  (includes photos of baskets for portfolio)
- ☐ Amortization
- ☐ Bank service charges
- ☐ Books and periodicals
  (includes subscriptions to industry magazines)
- ☐ Commissions paid to agents
- ☐ Consulting and other services
- ☐ Business conventions, conferences
  and trade organizations
- ☐ Dues to professional and trade associations
- ☐ Education and professional development,
  within limitations
- ☐ Electronic mail services
- ☐ Entertainment (percentage)
- ☐ Furniture and equipment
  (for the "basket room" and display)

- ☐ Insurance premiums
- ☐ Interest on business loans
- ☐ Legal fees
- ☐ License fees and taxes
- ☐ Local transportation
- ☐ Messenger services
- ☐ Office supplies
- ☐ Postage and shipping
- ☐ Printing and duplicating
- ☐ Repairs and maintenance on
  business equipment
- ☐ Telephone (within limitations)
- ☐ Travel out-of-town (includes
  tolls and parking)
- ☐ Wages and employee expenses

We advise that you consult an experienced tax adviser on all of the above for updated information and regulations as tax rules are constantly changing. Check with your local IRS office for the various publications available, i.e., Publication "334-Tax Guide for Small Business." Additionally ask them to send you Publication "910-Guide to Free Tax Services" and the publication titled "Your Business Tax Kit."

# Your Yearly Planner

*"Planning is the preparation for the events to come."*

— Don L. Price

**P**lanning is essential. Robert Schuller said "Yard by yard, life is hard; but inch by inch, it's a cinch." Plan correctly and coordinate inch by inch all of the events for a successful business.

You know about themes, holidays and special events. Now you must plan your inventory purchasing, marketing and selling in a chronological order. The best way to do this is to devise a yearly planner. Sit down with a month-at-a-glance calendar and use the sample planning schedule listed here to launch your business in the right direction.

---

# JANUARY
**Chart out your advertising objectives for the year**

- ☐ Low-cost advertising… Fliers, brochures, post cards, letters.
- ☐ Develop a free publicity campaign… Write a news article, donate to a community charity, get on a local radio talk program.
- ☐ Newspaper ads… Company newspapers, church newspapers, local and community newspapers.
- ☐ Business clubs… Attend your local chamber events and networking clubs
- ☐ Plan on attending… Fancy food or gourmet show, gift show, basket symposium, etc. Schedule them on your calendar!
- ☐ Make a new list of companies to call on this year — target your market.
- ☐ Have basket designs prepared for Lincoln's Birthday, Valentine's Day, Washington's Birthday and have inventory on hand.
- ☐ Prepare for President's Day.

**HOLIDAYS AND OTHER SPECIAL DAYS IN JANUARY**
**New Year's Day**
**Super Bowl**
**Martin Luther King Jr. Day**

# FEBRUARY

☐ Look through craft, decorating and decorative accessories magazines; study catalogs for new creative ideas and themes for your gift basket business.
☐ Make idea files for each holiday.
☐ Design, assemble and deliver Valentine gift baskets.
☐ Start planning and ordering products for Mother's Day and Easter.
☐ Have product on hand and design ideas for St. Patrick's Day.

**HOLIDAYS AND SPECIAL DAYS IN FEBRUARY**
**Lincoln's Birthday**
**Valentine's Day**
**Washinton's Birthday**
**Presidents' Day**

# MARCH

☐ Have secretaries' gift basket themes created.
☐ Send out fliers and brochures to targeted businesses and corporations.
☐ Make appointments to call on companies and corporate accounts for Secretaries' Day/Week.
☐ Have product available and designs ready for Easter business.
☐ Have a "Spring Fling" promotion. Present all your new spring colors in flowers, ribbons and other basket accessories.
☐ Start planning for Mother's Day.

**HOLIDAYS AND SPECIAL DAYS IN MARCH**
**St. Patrick's Day**

# APRIL

☐ Have baskets ready for Secretaries' Day/Week.
☐ Have products available and designs ready for Mother's Day.
☐ Start thinking about themes for June graduations.

**HOLIDAYS AND SPECIAL DAYS IN APRIL**
**April Fools' Day**
**Easter (or March)**
**Secretaries' Day/Week**

# MAY

- ☐ Have Mother's Day basket orders ready.
- ☐ Promote your wedding line of gift baskets in May for June weddings.
- ☐ Have basket themes created and send out fliers and brochures for Father's Day.

**HOLIDAYS AND SPECIAL DAYS IN MAY**
**Cinco de Mayo**
**Mother's Day**
**Memorial Day**

# JUNE

- ☐ Have Father's Day baskets ready for sale.
- ☐ Continue to promote your wedding gift baskets.
- ☐ Be creative with a summer promotion to clear out over-bought or unused merchandise. Have a summer "Blooming-Out Sale."
- ☐ Promote gift baskets for warm weather — seashore —using unbreakable pool accessories, pails, shovels, etc.
- ☐ Start your holiday idea and theme file for corporate accounts and develop ideas for your spectacular custom-designed holiday baskets.
- ☐ Start product sourcing for all items to be used in holiday baskets — work with different colors, ornaments and embellishments.

**HOLIDAY AND SPECIAL DAYS IN JUNE**
**Father's Day**
**Graduations & Weddings**

# JULY

**Time to review the first six months...**

- ☐ Did you meet or exceed goals?
- ☐ Did you make a profit?
- ☐ What do you need to change?
- ☐ Can your business grow faster, or do you need to slow down and take a break?
- ☐ Will you need to hire help to prepare for the big rush of the Thanksgiving and Christmas holiday season?
- ☐ Are you on target with advertising objectives and promotional campaigns?
  If not, now is the time to make corrections.
- ☐ Start purchasing holiday stock.
- ☐ Begin planning holiday promotions and marketing techniques — Open House, fliers, brochures, tasting party.

**HOLIDAYS AND SPECIAL DAYS IN JULY**
**Independence Day (Fourth of July)**

# AUGUST

- ☐ Take a vacation, enjoy the fruits of your labor.
- ☐ Attend a customer service seminar, sales seminar, gourmet food show, gift show or basket symposium.
- ☐ Continue to prepare for the holiday — purchasing product, planning Open House, promotions, corporate brochure.
- ☐ Have an end-of-summer sale. Clean out inventory room making way for winter holiday products.
- ☐ Plan Fall gift basket themes (Halloween, Thanksgiving) and purchase seasonal merchandise.

# SEPTEMBER

- ☐ Thanksgiving and Christmas are just around the corner… Good planning will help produce high profits.
- ☐ September and October are good months for promoting gift baskets for weddings and wedding showers.
- ☐ Have your holiday plans finalized. Have brochures ready for printer. List the corporate accounts to be contacted. Mail pre-season sales letters.

**HOLIDAYS AND SPECIAL DAYS IN SEPTEMBER**
**Labor Day**
**Grandparent's Day**
**Rosh Hashanah (or October)**
**Yom Kippur (or October)**

# OCTOBER

- ☐ Have portfolio ready — photographs and prices.
- ☐ Mail pre-approach sales letter with brochure to targeted companies.
- ☐ Make follow-up calls and appointments.
- ☐ Think about a tasting party for potential customers.
- ☐ Display at a craft fair or rent a kiosk in a shopping mall to promote your holiday gift baskets.
- ☐ If hiring extra help for the holidays, now is the time to train them well.
- ☐ Start taking those pre-holiday sales orders.

**HOLIDAYS AND SPECIAL DAYS IN OCTOBER**
**Columbus Day**
**Halloween**
**Boss's Day**

# NOVEMBER

- ☐ Have your special Thankgiving baskets displayed.
- ☐ Sell, Sell, Sell... Promote heavily with fliers, newspaper ads, personal calls to companies and existing clients.
- ☐ Close accounts for holiday corporate business.
- ☐ Begin assembling baskets for all Christmas orders.
- ☐ After November 31st, any corporate orders taken should have a price increase, or suggest sending baskets after holidays.
- ☐ Have enough inventory on hand to handle all your business.

**HOLIDAY AND SPECIAL DAYS IN NOVEMBER**
**Thanksgiving Day**
**Veterans' Day**
**Election Day**

# DECEMBER

- ☐ Continue assembling all gift baskets for the holidays.
- ☐ Have "Holiday Happening" to sell all consumer Christmas baskets.
- ☐ Deliver all corporate Christmas gift baskets.
- ☐ This is a good month to promote wedding baskets.
- ☐ Plan on working longer hours.
- ☐ Get in the spirit of the holiday season. Dress up in appropriate costumes and bring good cheer to your customers.

**HOLIDAYS AND SPECIAL DAYS IN DECEMBER**
**Hanukkah**
**Christmas Day**
**New Year's Eve**

NOTE: It is a good idea to encourage your corporate accounts to send baskets to their clients after the holiday rush (mid-January) for the following reasons:

1.  Gift baskets will be a welcome sight to their clients after all the stress of the Christmas season. At this "down-time" their clients will appreciate a lovely gift basket and it will stand alone without competition.

2.  It gives you more time to balance your work schedule and fulfill all orders in a timely manner. You will have more time for shopping, creating, shipping and selling.

Please advise the wholesalers and
manufacturers listed under
"Resources"
on the following pages,
that you obtained their name
from our book.
We appreciate your cooperation.

# Appendix B

# Resources

## ACCESSORY ITEMS

Wine Things Unlimited
P.O. Box 1349
Sonoma, CA 95476
800-447-3983
**wine gifts, accessories & gourmet foods**

Sniffs
112 Park Ave.
Wind Gap PA 18091
800-767-2368
**unique air fresheners**

Create A Gift Basket Intl.
2340 South El Camino Real, Suite 1
San Clemente, CA 92672
714-492-5104
**large selection of gift basket items—
excelsior, shrink wrap, gourmet foods,
baby & bath items**

Thymes Limited
420 N. 5th St. #1100
Minneapolis, MN 55401
800-869-0747
**lovely packaged bath preparations**

Seasons
P.O. Box 190460
Little Rock, Arkansas 72219-0460
800-533-6266
**fragrance items**

M.F. Surprises
3630 Fairmont Avenue
San Diego, CA 92105
800-368-9336
**lovely fragrance sheets**

Tender Heart Treasures Ltd.
10525 "J" St.
Omaha, NE 68217-1090
800-443-1367
**Victorian arts & crafts**

Mitchell's Beeswax Candles
12401 Folsom Blvd. Suite 204
Rancho Cordova, CA 954742
916-985-6136
**candles**

The Nome Company
7024 Arboreal Drive
Dallas, TX 75231
800-MR PIANO (1-800-677-4266)
**fantastic, romantic piano music**

Sarcastic Toy Company
520 California Blvd. 10
Napa, CA 94559
800-443-3894
**creative toy stuffed bears**

Old Print Factory, Inc.
P.O. Box 498
New Baltimore, Michigan 48047
800-325-5383
**die-cut greeting cards, stationery,
gift tags, calendars**

Aromatique, Inc.
P.O. Box 272
Heber Springs, AR 72543
800-262-7511
**potpourri**

## BASKETS

Albert Kessler & Co.
1355 Market Street
San Francisco, CA 94103-1383
800-KESSLER
**baskets, napkins, glassware & other**

Coe & Dru
6250 Boyle Ave.
Vernon, CA 90058
800-722-7538
**baskets**

Hsin Rong Imports
13516 Imperial Way
Santa Fe Springs, CA 90670
310-921-3838
**baskets**

Pacific Rim
5930 Fourth Ave. South
Seattle, WA 98108
206-767-5000
**baskets, florals, seasonal products**

Kuan Yuen Co.
12688 Ann St. Unit 1
Santa Fe Springs, CA 90670
310-903-9899
**baskets**

K&D Imports
25 Graphic Place
Moonachie, NJ 07074
800-543-NYNY
**baskets, silks, foliage, silk fruits**

Makato Imports, Inc.
P.O. Box 10325
Portland, OR 97210
503-226-2482
**baskets**

Palecek
P.O. Box 225
Station-A
Richmond, CA 94808
800-274-7730
**baskets & accessories**

Pioneer Wholesale Co.
500 W. Bagley Road
Berea, OH 44017
800-272-3454
**baskets**

Renies
1290 Pacific St
Union City, CA 94587
510-487-6919
**baskets and pottery**

Royal Cathay
2019 East Monte Vista Ave.
Vacaville, CA 95688
800-388-8890
**baskets, heat gun, etc.**

# BASKET FILLER

Fiberex, Inc.
P.O. Box 3003
Florence, AL 35630
800-243-3455

Windlestraw
135 Ten Rod Rd.
Exeter, RI 02822
800-225-8186
**excelsior, balloons, cello film,
shrink wrap, bows, baskets**

# CANDIES & CHOCOLATES

Harry London Candies, Inc.
1281 S. Main St.
North Canton, OH 44720-4299
800-321-0444
**celebration candies (new arrivals,
birthday, thank you, congratulations)**

David Alan Chocolatier
1700 North Lebanon St.
Lebanon, Indiana 46052-0588
800-428-2310
**premium chocolates (exquisite packaging)**

My Sister's Caramels
1884 Bret Hart
Palo Alto, CA 94303
800-735-2951, (415) 321-2582
**gourmet caramels**

Old Homestead Candies
8250 Old Homestead
Dallas, Texas 75217
800-398-6512
**peanut, almond, pecan, jalapeño,
macadamia crunch**

# CAKES, COOKIES

Grandma Pfeiffer
P.O. Box 1627
Lake Oswego, Oregon 97035
800-446-8574
**"cakes baked in a jar"**

Pacific Dessert Co.
420 E. Denny Way
Seattle, WA 98122
206-328-1950
**miniature tortes and puree**

Souffle de Paris
P.O. Box 1833
Laguna Beach, CA 92652-1833
714-499-6373
**assorted souffles, honeys, sauces**

Wamafuls INC.
800-552-1323
**certified kosher shortbread cookies
(unique packaging)**

La Tempesta Bakery
439 Littlefield Ave.
South San Francisco, CA 94080
415-873-8944
**biscotti**

San Anselmo Cookies
P.O. Box 2822
San Anselmo, CA 94979
800-229-1249
**San Anselmo biscotti (12 varieties)**

Golden Walnut Specialty Food
3840 Swanson Court
Gurnee, Illinois 60031
800-THE-FOIL
**unique specialty desserts (cheesecake,
pecan butterballs, cookies, etc.)**

# CHEESES, SAUSAGES, SALAMI

Heid Meat Service & Catering
W2012 Cty, Rd. JJ
Kaukauna, WI 54130
414-788-4888
**beer bottle salami, football & baseball
sausage, authentic beer labels (Bud,
Miller, etc.)**

Stauffer Cheese, Inc.
P.O. Box 68
Blue Mounds, WI 53517-0068
800-236-3300
**non-refrig cheese, sausage, preserves,
cookies**

Bongrain Cheese USA
400 S. Custer Ave.
New Holland, PA 17557
717-355-8549
**cheeses**

# COFFEE & TEA

Chicago Coffee Roastery, Inc
11880 Smith Court
Huntley, IL 60142
800-762-5402
**coffees**

F. Gaviña & Sons
2369 E. 51st St.
Vernon, CA 90058
800-428-4627
**gourmet coffees tastefully packaged**

Davidsons
P.O. Box 11214
Reno, NV 89510
800-882-5888
**teas, spices & accessories**

Provender International
6050 Blvd. E. Suite F, Lobby Level
West NY, NJ 07093
800-678-5603
**teas, jams, jellies, cookies,
salsa, candies**

# FLORALS

Coast
149 Morris Street
San Francisco, CA 94107
415-781-3034

Le Fleur Wholesale
800-201-SILK

Pacific Rim (see Baskets)
**florals**

# OTHER SPECIALTY FOODS

Buckeye Beans & Herbs
P.O. Box 28201
Spokane, WA 99228-8201
800-227-1686
**beans, soups, chilies, pasta mix,
bread mix**

Huckleberry Mountain
Box 3298
Jackson Hole, WY 83001
800-272-2999
**jams, jellies, dessert toppings,
pancake/waffle mix, choc. covered
popcorn, mini truffle, bon-bons**

The Just Tomatoes Co.
P.O. Box 807
Westley, CA 95387
800-537-1985
**dried tomatoes, fruit snacks, bell
peppers, greeting cards**

Pelican Bay Ltd.
639 Chestnut St.
Clearwater, FL 34616
800-826-8982
**mixes—dips, pasta, bake, mulling spices,
salsa, chili, herbs, salad dressings**

Canterbury Cuisine
P.O. Box 2271
Redmond, WA 98073
206-881-2555
**soups, mixes, dressing, dips, cakes,
muffins & bread**

Scott Farms
Route 3, Box 149B
Altus, OK 73521
405-482-1950
**mixes—dip, chili, cajun, popcorn,
gourmet beans, herbs & sauces,
S.W. jellies**

Ivy Cottage
709 Adelaine Ave.
South Pasadena, CA 91030
818-441-2761
**scone mix & fancy preserves**

Bettes Oceanview Diner
1807 A Fourth St.
Berkeley, CA 94710
510-644-3230
**breakfast products**

Kozlowski Farms
5566 Gravenstein Hwy N (116)
Forestville, CA 95436
800-473-2767
**jams, jellies, mustards, vinegars,
marmalades, BBQ & pasta sauce,
fudge sauce, salad dressings**

Lindsay Farms, Inc.
4794 Clark Howell Hwy, Bldg 3 & 4
Atlanta, GA 30349
404-305-0620
**jams, jellies, conserves, honeys, syrups,
condiments, southern mixes, confections,
cakes, chocolates, nuts**

The Brown Adobe
200 Lincoln Ave. Suite 130
Phoenixville, PA 19460
800-392-2041
**spicy specialties**

Pacific Gold Marketing Inc.
2910 Falcon Drive, Suite B
Madera, CA 93637
209-662-6176
**pistachios, cashews, other nuts &
confections**

Cortina Corporation
590 Noble Ave.
Van Nuys, CA 91411
800-828-3444/818-994-1888
**dessert toppings, wine mustards, pickled
condiments, salad dressings, oils,
vinegars, cookies, candies, nuts**

McStevens
P.O. Box 29
Clackamas, OR 97015
800-547-2803
**pancake, muffin, brownie mix, honey,
preserves, cocoas, milk coolers, steamers**

Squire Boone Village
P.O. Box 411
Corydon, IN 47112
800-234-1804
**popcorn, cake & cookie mixes, candles,
soap**

Poppin Cobs
1582 Browning
Irvine, CA 92714
714-261-7484
**popcorn on cob**

# Ribbon & Bows

CM Offray & Sons, Inc.
Route 24–Box 601
Chester, NJ 07930-0601
800-344-5533
**fabric & ribbon**

Rainbow Bows Inc.
P.O. Box 23185
Lansing, MI 48909-3185
800-727-BOWS
**multi-colored bows, ribbons**

# Seafood

Fort Chatham
632 N.W. 46th St.
Seattle, WA 98107
206-783-8200
**smoked seafood**

Alaska Smokehouse
21616 87th S.E.
Woodinville, WA 98072
800-422-0852
**custom-smoked salmon & spreads**

# Shrink Wrap

Crystal Vision Packaging Systems
21735 S. Western Ave.
Torrance, CA 90501
800-331-3240
**heat gun, shrink wrap**

Jetram Sales Inc
1430 MACKLIND AVE
ST. LOUIS, MO. 63110
800-551-2626
**heat gun, shrink wrap (and machines), basket kits, printed shrink film**

ATW Manufacturing Co. Inc.
4065 West 11th Avenue
Eugene, Oregon 97401
800-759-3388
**heat gun, shrink wrap & machines**

# Gardening Gifts and Environmentally-Friendly Product Companies

Applewood Seed Co.
5380 Vivian St.
Arvada, CO 80002
303-431-6283
**sof-pot planter kits**

Bandelier Designs, Inc.
2504 Camino Entrada
Santa Fe, NM 87505
505-474-0900
**note cards, stationery, journals, etc. printed on recycled paper**

Running Studio, Inc.
1020 Park St.
Paso Robles, CA 93446
800-235-4158
**unique tropical rainforest magnets**

Loose Ends
P.O. Box 20310
Salem, Oregon 97303
503-390-7457
**environmentally safe excelsior, giftwrap from recycled paper & other unique products**

Porta
131 Ethel Road W.
Piscataway, NJ 08854-5928
212-685-4241
**gardening accessories**

Savoy Bag Co.
920 Broadway, Suite #12
Woodmere, NY 11598
516-295-0061
**100% cotton, biodegradable, reusable shopping bags**

Gift Box Corporation
2330 No. 31st Ave.
Phoenix, AX 85009
800-GIFT BOX
**ecologically safe gift boxes, bags, bow machines, ribbons, totes, gift wrap**

The Paper Company
731 South Fidalgo
Seattle, Washington 98108
800-426-8989
**"EarthPaper" products & stationery from recycled paper**

Sarute
107 Horatio St.
New York, NY 10014
800-345-6404
**environmentally-sound packing materials**

Mud Pie
230 Spring St. Space 1633
Atlanta, Georgia 30303
404-523-6425
**bird feeders & other unique gardening accessories**

SS Sarna Inc.
65 Commerce Drive
Hauppauge, NY 11788
800-645-5844
**unique metal planters**

Sally's Choice
3814 4th Ave. S.
Seattle, WA 98134
800-683-SEED
**unique herb gardens, gardens in a book, etc.**

Opus
24 William Way
Box 525
Bellingham, MA 02019
508-966-0470
**bird feeders**

Community Products, Inc.
Rd #2, Box 1950
Montpelier, Vermont 05602
800-927-2695
**Rainforest crunch (cookies)**

Day Dream Publishing
4299 Carpinteria Ave.
Carpinteria, CA 93014-5020
**rainforest calendar printed on recycled papers**

Hen-Feathers & Co.
10 Balligomingo Road
Gulph Mills, PA 19428
215-828-1721
**gardening accessories**

Colors by Design
7723 Densmore
Van Nuys, CA 91406
800-832-8436
**gift wrap printed on recycled paper, greeting cards, invitations, etc.**

# SEMINARS, TRAINING AND CONSULTING

Camille Anderson
615 Esplanade #603
Redondo Beach, CA 90277
310-316-0611
**The Art of Creating Baskets, Advance Basket Designs**

Don L. Price & Associates
P.O. Box 7000-700
Redondo Beach, CA 90277
310-379-7797
**"Personal Marketing Power" The ultimate marketing tool—a 6-audio cassette program packed full of profitable tips & techniques on low-cost marketing for the home-based business of the '90s. Keynotes, Seminars, Consulting**

The Basket Affair Co.
525 NW Saltzman Rd.
Portland, OR 97229
800-243-2992
**basket seminars**

# PUBLICATIONS & OTHER RESOURCES

Gift Basket Resource Directory
18207 McDurmott East, Suite C
Irvine, CA 92714
800-833-4083
**comprehensive resource guide of suppliers & manufacturers**

The Yearbook by Barbara Wold
P.O. Box 9831
Newport Beach, CA 92658
714-854-9337
**The complete retail planner**

"Gift Basket Review"
Festivities Publications, Inc.
1205 Forsyth St.
Jacksonville, FL 32204-9912
904-634-1902
**monthly magazine of the gift basket industry**

Gifts & Decorative Accessories
51 Madison Avenue
New York, NY 10160-0376
212-532-0651
**business magazine of gifts, tabletop, gourmet, gift baskets, home accessories, greeting cards & stationery**

The Gourmet Retailer
3301 Ponce de Leon, Suite 300
Coral Gable, Florida 33134
800-397-1137
**industry magazine of specialty foods**

Gift & Stationery Business
1515 Broadway, 32nd floor
New York, NY 10036
800-964-9494
**magazine of gifts & stationery**

Giftware News
Civic Opera Bldg 20 N. Wacker St.
Suite 3230
Chicago, Illinois 60606
800-229-1967
**business magazine of giftware, stationery, gift baskets & tabletop**

Florist Review
P.O. Box 4368
Topeka, KS 66604
800-367-4708
**only independent florist magazine since 1897**

Fancy Food
Civic Opera Bldg. 20 N. Wacker St.
Suite 3230
Chicago, Illinois 60606
800-229-1967
**business magazine for the distribution & marketing of specialty foods & confections**

The Business of Sewing
Collins Publications
3233 Grand Ave. Suite N-294
Chino Hills, CA 91709
800-795-8999
**comprehensive step-by-step guide on starting, maintaining & achieving success in your own sewing business**

# VIDEOS

Those Bloomin' Baskets, etc.
615 Esplanade #603
Redondo Beach, CA 90277
310-316-0611
**"The Art of Creating Sensational Gift Baskets," Camille Anderson, co-author of this book & distinctive designer of gift baskets, shares her unique techniques and designs in this phenomenal, step-by-step video & valuable learning tool. (Available 1-1-94)**

# INDEX